BACKPACK Gold 4

Mario Herrera • Diane Pinkley

Contents

Backpack Song

It's time to open Backpack
 and see what we can see.
We'll have lots of adventures.
Explore Backpack with me!

Backpack is full of fun things
 we use each day in school.
Stories, puzzles, songs and games –
Backpack is really cool!

It's time to open Backpack
 and see what we can see.
We'll have lots of adventures.
Explore Backpack with me!

Backpack is full of fun and facts,
 projects and pictures, too.
We're learning English, we're never bored.
There are great new things to do!

It's time to open Backpack
 and see what we can see.
We'll have lots of adventures.
Explore Backpack with me!

1 Friends Old and New

1 Read. Listen and sing.

Is That You?

Is that you?
I think that you were in my class last year.
You were sitting there; I was sitting here.
But you don't look the same.

Your hair was shorter,
    and it was straight and brown.
Now your hair is longer,
    and curly all around!

Didn't you wear glasses?
And weren't your eyes blue?
Now you're so much taller,
    I can't believe it's you.

(Chorus)

Wow, you're really different,
    but I'm glad to see you, Millie.
What? That's not your name?
Now I feel really silly!

(Chorus)

Good to see you!

2   Physical appearance

2 Listen. Point and say.

1. Amanda's got long, straight blonde hair. She's got blue eyes.

2. Carmen's got short, curly brown hair. She's got brown eyes.

3. Harry's got short, straight red hair. He's got green eyes.

4. Lee's got straight dark hair and dark eyes. He wears glasses.

3 Listen and write in your notebook.

OUR NEW FRIENDS

1.   2.   3.   4.

Unit 1

Physical appearance

3

Our New Friends

4 Listen. Look and read.

Hi! I'm Lydia. This is a picture of me with my sister, Darlene. She's eight years old. I like helping her with her homework because I'm older than her. Sometimes I get impatient because she doesn't understand!

My name is Luis. Here I am at a football match with my dad. I love watching and playing football. When I sit on my dad's shoulders, I'm taller than the other boys. I get excited when my team wins the match!

Physical appearance; comparative adjectives; *get* + adjectives

Hi! We're twins. My sister's name is Pam, and my name is Dan. I'm a little shorter than my sister, but I am stronger. When we ride our bikes, I am always faster than Pam. Sometimes she gets angry because I win every race. But she's slow! Do you like riding bikes, too?

I'm Charlie. I love animals. I've got two kittens. Tabby is smaller and younger than Inky. They are friendly and fun to play with. Tabby and Inky get upset when I go to school.

TRACK A8

5 Point. Ask and answer.

> **Who is older? Lydia or Darlene?**

> **Lydia is older than Darlene.**

TRACK A9

6 Ask and answer.

> **When does Lydia get impatient?**

> **When her sister doesn't understand her homework.**

Unit 1

Question formation; comparative adjectives; *get* + adjectives

See Grammar Handbook **p. 111**

Grammar

Who is old**er**?	Lydia is old**er than** Darlene.	old → older
Who is young**er**?	Darlene is young**er than** Lydia.	young → younger

 Look and write.

big   small   old   young   short   tall

1. Fluffy is *bigger* than Whiskers. Whiskers is *smaller* than Fluffy.

2. Tony is ✳ ✳ ✳ than Jane. Jane is ✳ ✳ ✳ than Tony.

3. Timmy is ✳ ✳ ✳ than Mary. Mary is ✳ ✳ ✳ than Timmy.

Grammar

When do the kittens **get upset**?	They **get upset** when Charlie goes to school.	
When does he / she **get sad**?	He / She **gets sad** when his / her team loses.	

 Write questions or answers in your notebook.

Lucy

Sarah

1. Q. When does Bob get angry?

    A. ...

2. Q. ...

    A. She gets excited when her team wins the game.

3. Q. ...

    A. She gets impatient when Darlene doesn't understand.

Darlene

9 **Copy and complete the chart. Ask a friend.**

 When do you get scared?

 When I walk in the dark.

When do you get _____?	Me	My Friends
1. scared		
2. sad		
3. excited		
4. upset		
5. impatient		

Whose arm is longer?

Your arm is longer.

10 **Compare yourself to a friend.**

1. Who has got longer arms?
2. Who has got a longer neck?
3. Who has got smaller feet?
4. Who has got shorter hair?
5. Who is taller?

Friends Forever

Are You a Good Friend?

Answer 'yes' or 'no'.

1. I get excited when good things happen to my friends.
2. I listen to my friends when they've got problems.
3. I often do things my friends like doing.
4. I keep my friends' secrets.
5. I say I'm sorry if I get impatient or angry.

Our Readers' Letters

Dear Friends Forever,

Here is a photo of my best friend, Mary, and me. Can you guess who is who? Mary is taller than I am, and her hair is shorter than mine. She is stronger than I am, and she can run faster than I can. She is very friendly and nice. I help her with her homework sometimes, because I am better at maths and science than she is. At weekends, we love to ride our bikes in the park, and sometimes we go shopping together. We talk on the phone every day. I am so happy Mary is my best friend! I want to surprise her with our picture in your magazine!

Your reader,
Gina

Dear Friends Forever,

I am a new student at a new school in a new town. I miss my old friends. I don't know anybody here! How can I make some new friends?

All Alone

Dear All Alone,

It's hard starting at a new school, but be patient. You will make new friends. Smile, be friendly, and don't be shy. Go up to other children and introduce yourself. Join a sports team, play in the school band or join a club. Soon you will begin to meet people. And don't forget your old friends! Write to them and phone them once in a while. Keep pictures of your old friends in an album. That way, you can remember old times while you make new friends.

Fun with Friends!
Try to say these tongue twisters fast!

★ Five friends flee from five fat flies fast.

★ Someone sold Sheila six silver sandals.

★ Two terrible teams tripped on their toes.

★ Doug's double bubble gum bubbles double.

Word Fun

(1) Unscramble each of the words. Write each word in your notebook.

e s t p l a

(You put food on these.)

c e n l i p

(You write with this.)

s p i h c

(You eat these with a burger.)

(2) Make a word from these letters. Then use the word to complete the sentence below in your notebook.

d i h s p n i f r e

The secret of ✷ ✷ ✷ is being a good listener.

11 **Listen and match. Write the letters in your notebook.**

a

b

c

d

e

12 **Listen. Read and chant.**

A True Friend

A true friend is funny
   and makes you laugh.
A true friend shows you
   how to do maths.
A true friend remembers
   your birthday.
A true friend helps you
   in every way.
A true friend is kind
   and doesn't get sad.
A true friend listens
   when you feel bad.
What I'm saying
   is really true.
And there isn't a friend
   truer than you!

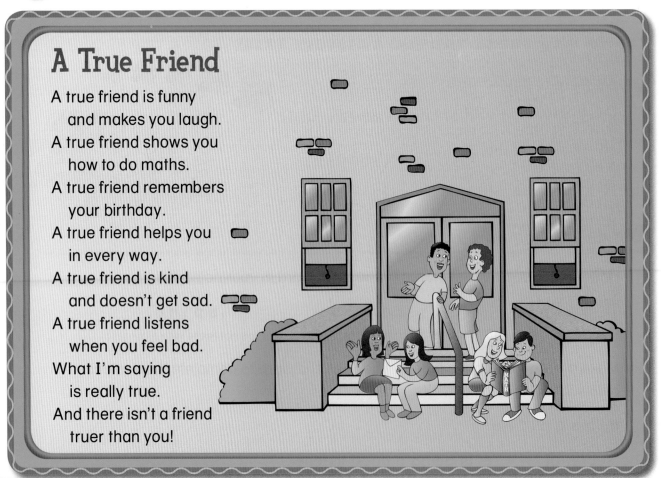

Listening for main ideas and details;
description; stress, rhythm and intonation

Conversation Cube

Cut out the cube on page 129 of your workbook.
Talk about family and friends.

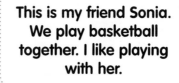

This is my friend Sonia. We play basketball together. I like playing with her.

Why?

She's a good player and she's taller than I am.

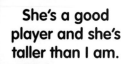

Be Friendly

Read and discuss.

Hi, I'm Mark, and I'm a new student at this school. It's hard to be a new student, because you don't know anybody and you have to make new friends. How? Be friendly.

Hi, I'm Lucy. I live here in this building. I have a new friend now! Her name is Nancy, and her family is moving into my building today. I like to meet new people.

1. Is it easy or hard for you to make friends?

2. How do you make new friends?

3. Do you like to have friends that are more like you or different from you? Why?

Know It? Show It!

Cut out the pictures on page 131 of your workbook. Take turns to describe the faces.

Have you got three in a row?

Choose a name. Compare your friend to you.

Sandra is younger than I am.

Unit 1

I can do it!

Unit 1

Performance assessment
See Assessment Package pp. 1–4, 7, 16 and 25–26.

13

TRACK A13

1 Read. Listen and sing.

Tommy's Week

On Monday Tommy makes his bed,
    as he does every day.
On Tuesday Tommy washes up,
    then puts the plates away.

On Wednesday Tommy practises
    his drums from five to six.
Then he cleans the garden path
    and picks up all the sticks.

On Thursday he takes out the rubbish,
    and sometimes sweeps the floor.
Tommy always thinks that
    a good son can do more.

On Friday Tommy goes to the shop
    for all his family's needs.
His mum and dad are proud of him
    for all of his good deeds.

When the weekend comes at last,
    to thank their helpful son,
they bring him home a video game,
    and join him in the fun.

What about
your week?

2 Listen. Read and say.

Sara: So, Jack, what are you doing this afternoon?

Jack: I've got to do my chores.

Sara: Me, too. What are you doing?

Jack: I'm looking after my little brother all afternoon. Then I'm washing the car for my dad.

Sara: Wow. That's a lot.

Jack: And what are you doing?

Sara: I'm shopping for food with my mother. After that, I'm helping her cook dinner.

What are Jack and Sara doing this afternoon?

3 Look and say.

Jack   Sara

TRACK A16
4 Listen. Look and read.

Busy people have full schedules.

Paul likes all sports, but he plays football in his free time. He has football practice twice a week and a match every Saturday. That means he plays football three times a week. What a busy schedule!

Naomi likes playing chess in her free time. She's in the chess club at school. The chess club meets once a week, on Monday afternoons from 3.00 to 4.30 in the school cafeteria. Naomi was very glad to meet other students who like playing chess.

Routines; expressions of frequency

Leo sings with a group called The Tones. To be in The Tones, you have to have a good voice. You also have to stay after school twice a week to practise. Leo never misses practice. He fits practice time into his schedule because he really loves singing.

Robert plays the drums in his free time. He practises every day for 30 minutes. He usually practises when he gets home from school. Most of his neighbours aren't home at that time, so Robert can play his drums very loudly.

TRACK A17

5 Point. Ask and answer.

What does Paul do in his free time?

He plays football.

TRACK A18

6 Ask and answer.

How often does Paul play football?

Three times a week.

Question formation; expressions of frequency

Unit 2

17

See Grammar Handbook p. 112

Grammar

	he / she	do in	his / her	free time?	He / She	plays football.
What does						
What do	you / they	do in	your / their	free time?	I / They	play chess.

7 **Write questions or answers in your notebook.**

1. Q. What does he do in his free time?
   A. *He plays tennis.*

2. Q. What does she do in her free time?
   A. ...

3. Q. What do they do in their free time?
   A. ...

4. Q. ...
   A. He sings with The Tones.

5. Q. ...
   A. I ride my bike.

play tennis

make jewellery

collect sports cards

Grammar

	he / she	play football?		Every Friday.	at weekends once a month twice a year
How often does					
How often do	you / they	sweep the floor?		On Sundays.	once a week three times a week

8 **Read the chart. Answer the questions.**

		Sunday	Monday	Tuesday	Wednesday	Thursday	Friday	Saturday
Emil	make/bed	x						x
Jan	wash/car			x				
Sue	shop/food		x		x		x	

1. How often does Emil make his bed?

2. How often does Jan wash the car?

3. How often does Sue shop for food?

Information questions; expressions of frequency See Grammar Handbook page 112.

Ask four friends. Tell the class.

> What chores do you do at home?

> How often do you wash up?

> I wash up.

> Twice a week.

Name	Chore	How Often
Ken	washes up	twice a week
*	* * *	* * *
*	* * *	* * *
*	* * *	* * *
*	* * *	* * *

10 What are you doing this weekend? Write in your notebook. Compare your list with a partner's.

> I'm playing basketball this weekend.

Kids' Corner Magazine

Cows Have Got Good Taste

(And we're not talking about roast beef!)

Cows like classical music better than rock and roll. How do we know? Daniel McElmurray, 10, helps his father to milk their cows every afternoon. He and his dad usually listen to music when they do this job. When Daniel needed an idea for a science project, he thought of the cows. He was curious. What kinds of music did cows like? He played rock and roll, folk and classical music for them. The cows gave a lot more milk with classical music. The cows were happy, and Daniel won first prize for his project!

Next Month:
Five Great Things to do This Summer!

You know you need glasses when . . .

What do you do in your free time?

Ask Alicia

Dear Alicia,

   My younger brother always forgets to do his chores. He has to feed our cat Wilma every day and water the plants twice a week. When he forgets, poor Wilma gets hungry and the plants turn brown. When I ask him about his chores, he gets angry. I don't want Wilma to be hungry, but I haven't got time to feed her. Why? Because I'm washing up and taking out the rubbish every night. Help!

Worried

Dear Worried,

   Try this idea. Swap chores with your brother. You can take care of the cat and the plants, and he can wash up and take out the rubbish. That way your cat and your plants will live. Good luck!

New Contest!

Are You Mother's Little Helper?

Do you help around the house?
What chores do you do?
How often do you do them?

Free Time Photo Album

Anna works in the garden in her free time.

Jason plays his guitar for children in hospital.

11 Listen and match. Write the letters in your notebook.

 **a**

 **b**

 **c**

 **d**

 **e**

12 Listen. Read and chant.

A Kid's Life

We ride scooters or kick a ball.
We go shopping at the mall.
We read books and magazines.
We look at computer screens.
We climb oak trees or play jacks.
We eat yummy, healthy snacks.
Just when we are having fun
     come the chores that must be done:
Clean your bedroom! Feed the cat!
Put away your rounders bat!
Do we always do these tasks?
Yes. We do as mother asks!

Listening for main ideas and details; stress, rhythm and intonation

My Schedule

Draw pictures of weekly activities.

Social Studies Project

What do you do on Tuesdays?

I play football. I play twice a week, on Tuesdays and Saturdays.

Content connection: social studies; art

Work and Play

Read and discuss.

Children need time to play. Play helps children to develop their minds, bodies and social skills. Play is important for learning about people and the world. And play is fun!

Children need to work some of the time, too. Why? Work is another way to learn about the world. Doing work helps children to understand responsibility. Typical examples of work that children can do include doing homework, helping around the house and taking care of their brothers and sisters.

1. What are your favourite ways to play?

2. Do you have some work or chores to do? Explain.

3. Do you think children need to work and play, or just play? Why?

Know It? Show It!

Cut out the cards on page 131 of your workbook.
Ask and answer.

When do you clean your room?

I clean my room at the weekend.

Make a collage of your free-time activities.

I go skateboarding in the park on Saturdays.

Mark's Free-Time Activities

Skateboarding

riding my bike

swimming   music

Comic Book

Comics

ticket

films

Unit 2

I can do it!

Unit 2

Performance assessment
See Assessment Package pp. 1–4, 8, 17 and 25–26.

25

3 At the World's Table

What's That?

What is that on your plate?
It looks and smells so great!
I would like to try some!
(Repeat)

Would you like to try some?
It's a Korean recipe.
It's hot and spicy cabbage.
It's really good, you'll see!

And would you like to try some?
It's a Mexican recipe.
It's made with rice and chicken.
Oh try some now, you'll see!

(Chorus)

Would you like to try some?
It's a Moroccan recipe
    with peppers and tomatoes.
It's really good, you'll see!

And would you like to try some?
It's an Italian recipe.
It's pasta cooked with meatballs.
Oh try some now, you'll see!

(Chorus)

2 Listen. Read and say.

Waiter: Good afternoon. Are you ready to order?

Ann: Yes. I'll have a bowl of vegetable soup and a cheese sandwich.

Waiter: Would you like anything to drink?

Ann: Yes. I'd like a can of cola.

Waiter: And you? What would you like?

Pat: I'd like a burger and some chips, please.

Waiter: And to drink?

Pat: Have you got any fruit juice?

Waiter: There isn't any juice left. Sorry.

Pat: Well, just some water, then.

Waiter: OK. I'll bring your drinks right now.

What would they like?

3 Listen and say.

Mary

Paul

4 **Listen. Look and read.**

People in different countries eat many of the same foods. They prepare them in different ways and eat them at different times of day.

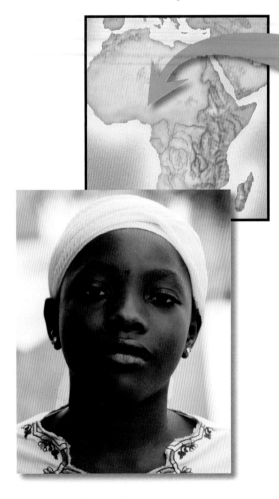

Nigeria, Africa

My favourite breakfast is a fried ball of bean paste with a chilli pepper in the centre (*akara*). It wakes you up! For lunch, I have rice and soup with meat and vegetables. For dinner, my favourite dish is a kind of stew with fish and onions. I eat it with mashed yam and plantain (*fufu*). It's delicious!

Ireland, Europe

Breakfast is a big meal in my house. I have cereal with milk and then eggs and toast with jam. For lunch, I like *colcannon,* a dish made with potatoes, cabbage, onions and cream. I eat lamb or roast beef for dinner. On special occasions, I have Dublin *coddle,* a meat stew with onions and potatoes. Yum!

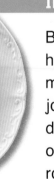

Food; *like* + noun

For breakfast, I have a bowl of rice, soup and some grilled fish. I always have some pickles, too. Lunch at school is usually noodles, tofu and curry rice. At home, my favourite lunch is some raw fish (*sushi*). For dinner, I eat rice mixed with ketchup and chicken inside an omelette. I like some *natto,* too. It's a sticky dish made from soya beans. It tastes great!

TRACK A27

5 **Point. Ask and answer.**

What does she like for breakfast?

She likes bean paste with a chilli pepper in it.

TRACK A28

6 **Ask and answer.**

Would you eat a chilli pepper for breakfast?

No, I wouldn't, but I'd eat bean paste.

Question formation; *like* + noun; *would* + verb

See Grammar Handbook → **p. 113**

Grammar

What **would** you **like**?	**I'd like** a bowl of soup.	I'd like → I would like
What **would** he / she **like**?	He'd / She'd **like** a sandwich.	He'd like → He would like
		She'd like → She would like

 Complete the sentences.

1. Good afternoon. What ✳ ✳ ✳ you ✳ ✳ ✳ ?

2. I ✳ ✳ ✳ a burger and chips, please.

3. She ✳ ✳ ✳ some fruit salad.

4. He ✳ ✳ ✳ some pizza.

Grammar

Would	you he she	**try** noodles?	Yes,	I he she	**would**.	No,	I he she	**wouldn't**.

 Complete the sentences.

1. ✳ ✳ ✳ you try a chilli pepper?

   Yes, I ✳ ✳ ✳ .

2. ✳ ✳ ✳ Julia eat a chilli pepper?

   No, she ✳ ✳ ✳ . She doesn't like spicy food.

3. ✳ ✳ ✳ Tim drink cola?

   No, he ✳ ✳ ✳ . He doesn't like cola.

Information questions; *would like* + noun;
contractions See Grammar Handbook page 113.

9 **Look at the menu and write in your notebook.**

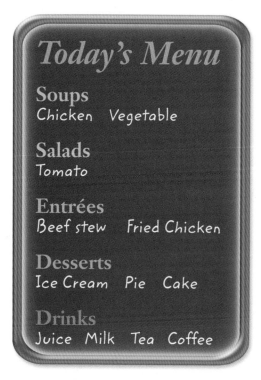

Today's Menu

Soups
Chicken   Vegetable

Salads
Tomato

Entrées
Beef stew   Fried Chicken

Desserts
Ice Cream   Pie   Cake

Drinks
Juice   Milk   Tea   Coffee

1. Is there any spaghetti on the menu?

   No, there isn't any.

2. Is there any tomato salad?

3. Are there any desserts on the menu?

4. Is there any lemonade?

10 **Work with a partner. You are a waiter or a customer in a café.**

Good Times Café

Soups and Salads
Tomato Soup	£2.50	Lettuce and
Chicken Soup	£2.50	Tomato Salad £4.50

Sandwiches
Cheese	£2.95	Burger £3.25
Chicken	£3.50	Cheeseburger £3.75
Tuna	£3.25	Veggie Burger £3.75

Side Orders
Potato Crisps	£1.00	Chips £1.50
Beans	£1.00	Pickles £0.50

Desserts
Vanilla Ice Cream	£1.50	Apple Pie £2.50
Chocolate Ice Cream	£1.50	Cheesecake £3.00

Drinks
Apple Juice	£1.25	Cola £1.50
Orange Juice	£1.25	Milkshake £2.00

What would you like?

I'd like a tuna sandwich and some chips, please.

Food Facts and Fun
A Magazine for Food Fans

Q: What's a food pyramid?

A: A food pyramid shows the different food groups. It tells us how much to eat to stay in good health. Use the food pyramid to help you eat well.

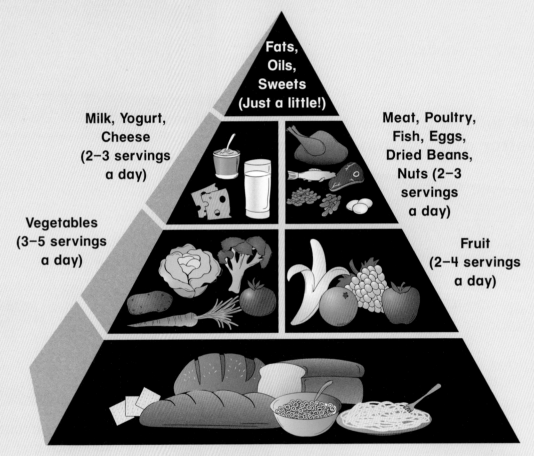

Fats, Oils, Sweets (Just a little!)

Milk, Yogurt, Cheese (2–3 servings a day)

Meat, Poultry, Fish, Eggs, Dried Beans, Nuts (2–3 servings a day)

Vegetables (3–5 servings a day)

Fruit (2–4 servings a day)

Bread, Rice, Cereal, Pasta (6–11 servings a day)

A man goes to the doctor. He's got a carrot in one ear and a banana in the other ear. He says to the doctor, "Doc, I don't feel very well". The doctor looks at him and says, "Of course you don't. You're not eating properly!"

Food Myths

TRUE or FALSE ???

★ Chocolate is bad for your skin.

★ A typical person from the UK eats 35,000 biscuits in a lifetime.

★ Watermelon seeds can grow inside your stomach.

★ Smelling apples or bananas every day can help you lose weight.

★ Carrots are good for your eyes.

★ Pineapples come from pine trees.

Play with Your Food Contest Winners!

1st Prize
Elsa Alvarez

2nd Prize
Khalid Arifi

3rd Prize
Jane Hunter

Food Fun: Make a Vegetable Print

1. Cut a potato, an onion and a piece of celery in half.

2. Cut shapes into each half of the potato.

3. Use the natural pattern of the onion and celery.

4. Use ink pads with coloured ink or put paint on a paper plate.

5. Press the vegetables into the ink or paint.

6. Make a border around a piece of paper. Now you have your own picture frame, card or paper to write letters on!

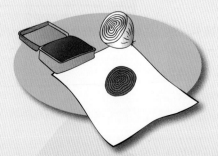

11 **Listen. Write T for *true* and F for *false* in your notebook.**

12 **Listen. Read and chant.**

I Don't Want To!

Now don't be silly, try it.
Just one spoonful, taste it.
If you try this green pea soup,
   you'll see how much you like it!

Now come on, have a taste.
There's no more time to waste.
If you try this meatball now,
   you'll see you like the taste!

Now come on, have a bite.
Let's not take all night.
If you try this fresh seafood,
   you'll know it tastes just right!

Now don't be silly, try it.
Just one mouthful, taste it.
If you try this special cheese,
   you'll see how much you like it!

Listening for the main idea and details; food;
stress, rhythm and intonation

Place Mat

Make a place mat about a country and its food.

People eat a lot of seafood in Ecuador. Ceviche is a typical dish. It is raw fish with lots of lime juice.

Content connection: social studies; art

Eat Wisely

Read and discuss.

It is very important to have a good breakfast every day. Having breakfast in the morning gives you energy to start the day.

Choose snacks that are good for your health, such as fruit or a sandwich. Eating food with too much sugar or too much fat is bad for you.

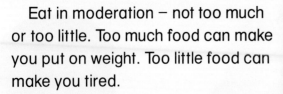

Eat in moderation — not too much or too little. Too much food can make you put on weight. Too little food can make you tired.

1. Do you always have breakfast? What do you have for breakfast?

2. What are your favourite snacks? Are they good or bad for you?

3. Why is it important to eat the right amount of food and not too much or too little?

Know It? Show It!

Cut out the cards on page 135 of your workbook.
Ask and answer.

> **Would you eat octopus?**

> **No, I wouldn't. I don't like seafood.**

You are in a restaurant. Role-play.

> **I'd like a bowl of tomato soup, please.**

Unit 3

I can do it!

Performance assessment
See Assessment Package pp. 1–4, 9, 18 and 25–28.

TRACK A32

1 Read. Listen and sing.

Good Advice

Let me give you some good advice.
Don't make me say it twice.
Take care, or you'll pay the price!

You shouldn't ride your bike today.
You lost your helmet yesterday.
You could hurt yourself in a fall,
    and you may never ride your bike at all.

Meg shouldn't always stay up late.
She knows her school bus comes at eight.
She'll enjoy herself late tonight,
    but tomorrow morning Meg will not feel right.

(Chorus)

Kids shouldn't stay in the sun all day.
Suncream and hats make it safe to play.
But if they burn themselves in the sun,
    later on they won't be having fun. Ouch!

Al shouldn't run so fast, you know.
The pavement's full of ice and snow.
He could fall or trip, slip and slide,
    and he will end up right on his backside!

(Chorus)

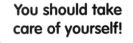

You should take care of yourself!

2 Listen. Read and say. What's the matter?

1. **A:** I've got toothache.

   B: You should go to the dentist.

2. **A:** I've got earache.

   B: You should go to the doctor.

3. **A:** I've got a headache.

   B: You should take some aspirin.

4. **A:** I've got stomach ache.

   B: You should drink some of this tea.

5. **A:** I've got a bad cold.

   B: You should drink lots of water and rest in bed.

3 Look and say.

What's the matter?

earache

cold

stomach ache

toothache

TRACK A35

4 Listen. Look and read.

Everyone should exercise for 30 minutes or more every day. There are many fun ways to keep in shape.

Go for a Walk

Going for a walk with family or friends is fun. Take a bottle of water with you and remember to wear comfortable shoes. Walking quickly is good for your heart.

Play a Sport

Play a sport like football. You should warm up and stretch before you practise or play in a game. Wear equipment to protect yourself. If you don't, you could get hurt. Playing football is good for your muscles.

Do Yoga

Practise yoga to learn breathing exercises and body postures. Yoga helps you stay healthy and in focus. It's good for your body and mind.

Health vocabulary; *should* + verb; reflexive pronouns

Skipping

Skipping is great exercise. You can skip by yourself or with friends. Skipping is good for your heart and muscles.

Swim

Swimming in a pool or in the sea is a lot of fun. Always swim with another person and remember to use suncream on sunny days to protect your skin. Swimming exercises all the muscles in the body.

TRACK A36

5 **Point. Ask and answer.**

What should I do to take care of myself?

You should go for a walk every day.

TRACK A37

6 **Ask and answer.**

Why should people go for walks?

Because walking is good for your heart.

Question formation; *should* + verb; reflexive pronouns

Grammar

See Grammar Handbook **p. 114**

I		myself.	He		himself.
You		yourself.	She	takes care of	herself.
We	take care of	ourselves.			
You		yourselves.			
They		themselves.			

7 Look and write in your notebook. Use *himself, ourselves, themselves* or *yourself.*

I.

 2.  3.  4.

1. Be careful! Don't hurt ✳ ✳ ✳ .

2. We love playing football. We enjoy ✳ ✳ ✳ a lot.

3. They've got suncream to protect ✳ ✳ ✳ .

4. Tell him to warm up and stretch, or he could hurt ✳ ✳ ✳ .

Grammar

I			I		
You			You		
He	**should** swim with others.		He	**shouldn't** swim alone.	
She			She		
We			We		
They			They		

8 Copy and complete the sentences. Use *should* or *shouldn't.*

1. You ✳ ✳ ✳ drink tea for your stomach ache.

2. Bob and Pat ✳ ✳ ✳ be outside playing. They have colds.

3. Sarah ✳ ✳ ✳ go to the doctor for her earache.

4. Karen ✳ ✳ ✳ stay up so late.

Reflexive pronouns; *should* + verb
See Grammar Handbook page 114.

9 Ask three friends. Copy the chart into your notebook. Give advice.

I drank two glasses of water yesterday.

You should drink more water!

Name	How much water did you drink yesterday?	How much time did you exercise yesterday?	How many hours of sleep did you get last night?	How many times did you brush your teeth yesterday?
Suzanne	2 glasses	30 minutes	8 hours	3 times
1.				
2.				
3.				

10 How do you take care of yourself? Talk with a partner.

Simple past; should + verb; health

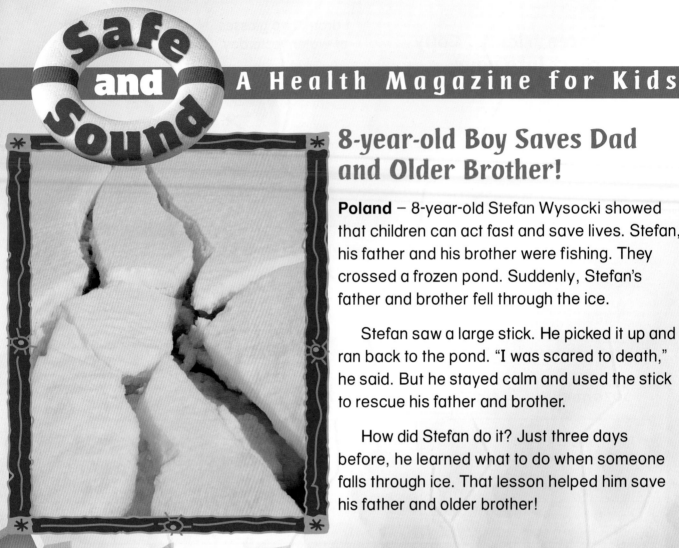

8-year-old Boy Saves Dad and Older Brother!

Poland – 8-year-old Stefan Wysocki showed that children can act fast and save lives. Stefan, his father and his brother were fishing. They crossed a frozen pond. Suddenly, Stefan's father and brother fell through the ice.

Stefan saw a large stick. He picked it up and ran back to the pond. "I was scared to death," he said. But he stayed calm and used the stick to rescue his father and brother.

How did Stefan do it? Just three days before, he learned what to do when someone falls through ice. That lesson helped him save his father and older brother!

Emergency Phone Numbers

Write these numbers in your notebook.

Family (work) _____

Family (home) _____

Police _____

Fire _____

Ambulance _____

Hospital _____

DID YOU KNOW?

Bike accidents are a top reason children go to hospital!

Be prepared! What should your first-aid kit have?

- ✓ aspirin
- ✓ bandages
- ✓ blanket
- ✓ burn cream
- ✓ gauze
- ✓ ice pack
- ✓ safety pin
- ✓ scissors
- ✓ antiseptic
- ✓ thermometer

Our Readers Want to Know . . .

Dear Safe and Sound,
I'm curious. What are the illnesses that make children miss school?

Frank Webb

Dear Frank,

Our *Safe and Sound Survey* of school nurses and parents shows that the number one reason children miss school is because they've got flu or a bad cold. In second place are diseases such as chicken pox. In third place are accidents such as broken legs, arms and ankles. In fourth place is stomach ache, and in fifth place is earache.

THE JOKE CORNER

A: I never get a summer cold!

B: How do you do that?

A: I catch it in the winter!

A: What's the best time to eat breakfast?

B: Before lunch!

A: What runs but never gets tired?

B: Water!

It's a Fact!

Many children's visits to hospital could be prevented by using safety equipment like helmets.

11 Listen and match. Write the letters in your notebook.

a

b

c

d

e

12 Listen. Read and chant.

Who's Sorry Now?

Look at Tommy, ill in bed.
He didn't do what his mother said.
He left all the vegetables on his plate,
    ate sweets at night and stayed up late.

Look at Cathy, ill in bed.
She didn't do what her doctor said.
She's got a cold. Her throat is sore.
Now she's got a fever, headache and more.

I'm not home and ill in bed.
I'm outside with my friends instead.
I'm feeling great. I'm feeling fine.
I take care of this body of mine.

Listening for main idea and details; health;
stress, rhythm and intonation

Safety Rules Mural

Cut out the stars on page 137 of your workbook.

You should always wear a seat belt.

Content connection: social studies; health; art

Stay Healthy

Read and discuss.

Wash your hands to stay healthy. Everything you touch has different kinds of germs. Wash your hands with soap because soap kills many of the germs that can make you ill. Do this several times a day.

When you eat sweets, cake or ice cream, it is important to brush your teeth afterwards. The sugar in these foods stays in your mouth and helps bacteria grow. For strong teeth brush your teeth after meals and snacks.

1. When do you wash your hands? How often do you wash your hands?

2. How many times a day do you brush your teeth?

3. Why is it important to wash your hands and brush your teeth regularly?

Know It? Show It!

Play a game.

> You should use soap and water to clean the cut.

Start ►

★ **Finish**

Do an advertisement for a health product.

> You should try Cold Away. Cold Away is a great way to take care of yourself.

Unit 4

I can do it!

Unit 4

Performance assessment
See Assessment Package pp 1–4, 10, 19 and 25–26.

49

Dinosaur Days

Dinosaurs, dinosaurs,
  what do we know?
What were they like,
  and where did they go?

Some were huge,
  some were smaller.
Some were short,
  and some were taller.

Some were fast,
  and some were slow.
They lived many millions
  of years ago.

Some walked on two legs,
  some walked on four.
They had long names
  like plesiosaur.

Some ate plants,
  some ate meat.
I think dinosaurs
  are really great!

What do you know about dinosaurs?

2 Listen. Point and say.

7 tonnes   38 tonnes

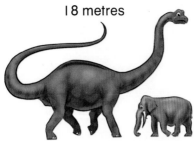

18 metres

7 metres

smaller   small

1. Some dinosaurs were heavier than others.

2. Many dinosaurs were bigger than an elephant.

3. Some dinosaurs were smaller than a hen.

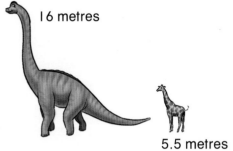

16 metres

5.5 metres

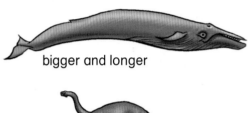

bigger and longer

big and long

4. Many dinosaurs were taller than a giraffe.

5. But the blue whale is longer and bigger than any of the dinosaurs.

3 Point and say.

1.
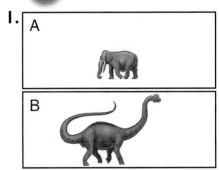

A

B

bigger

2.
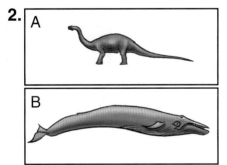

A

B

longer and bigger

3.
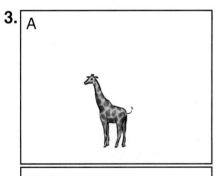

A

B

taller

4.

A

B

smaller

5.
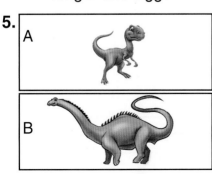

A

B

heavier

4 **Listen. Look and read.**

Extinct Animals

Dinosaurs lived for more than 160 million years! Some dinosaurs ate only plants, and some ate other animals. Some dinosaurs were bigger than an elephant. But about 65 million years ago, the dinosaurs died out or became extinct. Maybe an asteroid hit the Earth and made it too cold for the dinosaurs to live.

Dinosaurs are not the only animals that died out. In January 2000, the last Pyrenean ibex died in Spain. Scientists aren't sure why it did not survive. Some say it was because of overhunting. Others believe its habitat disappeared little by little.

Endangered Animals

Today there are animals in danger of becoming extinct. The giant panda is in trouble. People are cutting down the bamboo forests that provide its food. Pandas need a lot of food because they are big and heavy.

The Komodo dragon is also endangered. It is a very large reptile that lives on a few small islands of Indonesia. It is in danger because people are hunting it. Also, it is losing its habitat.

TRACK A45
 5 Point. Ask and answer.

TRACK A46
 6 Ask and answer.

> **What happened to the dinosaurs?**

> **They died out. The weather got too cold.**

> **What is happening to giant pandas today?**

> **Giant pandas are in danger. People are cutting down the bamboo forests.**

Grammar

See Grammar Handbook p. 115

What does the panda eat?	The panda eats bamboo.
When did dinosaurs live?	Dinosaurs lived more than 65 million years ago.
Where does the panda live?	The panda lives in China.
How long is a blue whale?	A blue whale is longer than any dinosaur.

 Write questions in your notebook.

Endangered Animals

leatherback turtle   Przewalski's horse   giant armadillo

1. Q. ... ?
   Leatherback turtles come on land to lay their eggs.

2. Q. ... ?
   A. Today Przewalski's horses live only in zoos.

3. Q. ... ?
   A. The giant armadillo grows up to 1.5 metres in length and weighs up to 55 kilos.

Grammar

Why did Pyrenean ibexes die out?	They died out **because** people hunted them too much.
Why are Asian lions endangered?	They're endangered **because** people are moving into their habitat.

 Write answers in your notebook.

1. Why did dinosaurs die out?

2. Why are Komodo dragons endangered?

3. Why are giant pandas endangered?

A. Choose an animal. Write four questions in your notebook.

1. What ... ?

2. Why ...?

3. Where ... ?

4. How ... ?

B. Make a chart like this in your notebook. Ask the questions to four friends. Tick their correct answers.

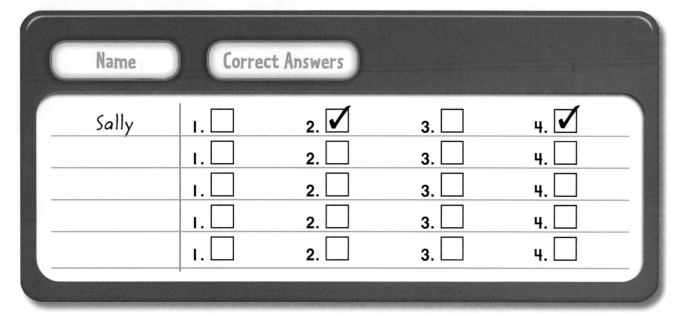

Name	Correct Answers			
Sally	1. ☐	2. ✔	3. ☐	4. ✔
	1. ☐	2. ☐	3. ☐	4. ☐
	1. ☐	2. ☐	3. ☐	4. ☐
	1. ☐	2. ☐	3. ☐	4. ☐
	1. ☐	2. ☐	3. ☐	4. ☐

10 Work in groups. Talk about why some animals are extinct or endangered.

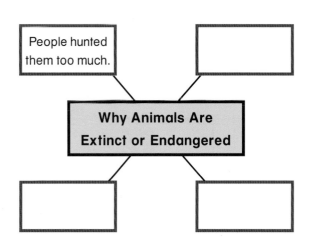

People hunted them too much.

Why Animals Are Extinct or Endangered

Some animals died out because people hunted them too much.

Yes. Like leatherback turtles.

And I think that's why some animals are endangered.

Unit 5

Animal Tracks Magazine

for kids who are wild about animals

You're Our Star, Erica!

How did a 12-year-old help endangered animals and work with stars at the same time? Two years ago, Erica Summers started a toy animal company, Stars in the Wild! First, Erica and her dad designed a toy animal. Then Erica went right to the stars – Hollywood film stars. She asked for their help. And they said yes! Many stars have got Erica's animals. Money from the sale of each toy animal helps endangered animals. Christina Aguilera bought a polar bear. Mandy Moore bought a koala. Other stars bought white tigers, harp seals, black leopards and gorillas.

Animal Limericks

There was a young lady from Niger,
who smiled as she rode on a tiger.
They returned from the ride
with the lady inside,
and a smile on the face of the tiger.

There once was a huge dinosaur,
who lived very close to the shore.
He wanted to swim,
but when he went in,
the water wasn't there any more.

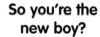
So you're the new boy?

Animal Drawing Contest Winners

There were so many entries to choose from. Here are the winners.

leopard

koala: endangered

First Prize
Mary Carter, age 11,
Birmingham, UK

Second Prize
Juan Cruz, age 10,
Toledo, Spain

Fascinating **Animal Facts**

A camel has SIX eyelids, three on each eye!

Questions from Our Readers

How many kinds of animals are there?
More than one million!

Which animals move from place to place?
Fish, whales, birds, insects and some land animals travel from one place to another.

Why do animals move around?
To find food, a good place to have babies, or better weather.

How do the animals find their way?
On land, some animals use mountains or valleys to show them the way. The flavour of the water guides green turtles! Other animals use stars and planets to guide them.

11 Listen and match. Write the numbers and letters in your notebook.

1. There are   C   kinds of rhinoceros.
   a. two   **b.** three   **c.** five

2. Rhinos live in ∗ .
   a. Africa and Asia   **b.** Asia and Europe

3. Black rhinos and white rhinos have got ∗ horns.
   a. no   **b.** two   **c.** three

4. Rhinos in India and Java have got ∗ .
   a. no horns   **b.** one horn   **c.** two horns

5. Rhinos are endangered because people hunt them for ∗ .
   a. their meat   **b.** their skin   **c.** their horns

12 Listen. Read and chant.

Animals All Around

Animals are all around us,
   they're around us every day.
But, like the ancient dinosaurs,
   some might go away.

We must protect the planet
   for animals large and small.
They need clean air and water
   to have a chance at all.

Animals need their habitats
   to eat and grow and thrive.
If their habitats disappear,
   these groups may not survive.

Some animals are in danger,
   in danger of dying out.
But this is a problem in nature
   we *can* do something about!

green turtle

kiwi bird

orangutan

Listening for the main idea and details;
stress, rhythm and intonation

Animal Sculpture

Create an animal that won't die out.

What does your animal eat?

Plants and leaves from trees. Where does your animal live?

Content connection: science; art

Protect Animals

Read and discuss.

Help animals by finding a group that supports protection for animals and their habitats. Help this group by giving money or giving your time. Another way to help is to talk to people in the neighbourhood about protecting animals of the world.

All animals need proper care and protection. Care for your pets and for other animals. Be sure they have food and water and a safe place to stay. Keep animal habitats clean for healthy animals.

1. Are there groups and organisations that protect animals in your town?

2. Do you help protect animals and their habitats? How?

3. Why is it important to protect animals?

Know It? Show It!

Spin. Ask and answer.

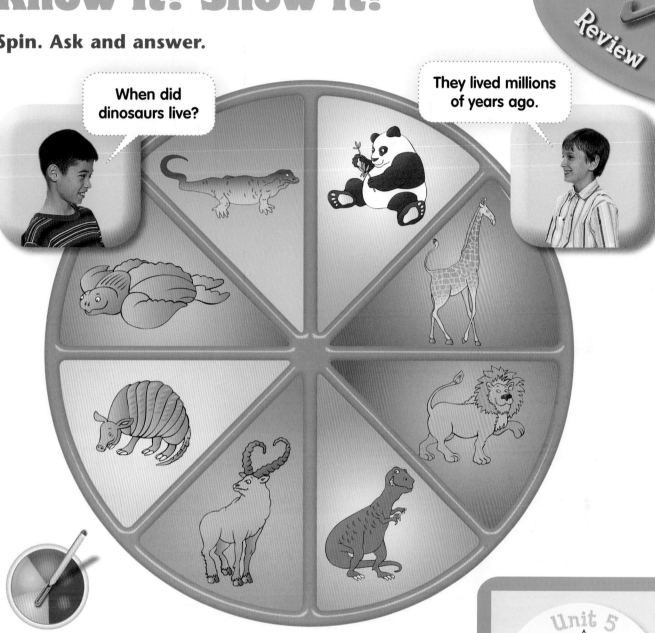

When did dinosaurs live?

They lived millions of years ago.

Make endangered animal cards.

This card shows an orangutan.

It's endangered because people are cutting down trees.

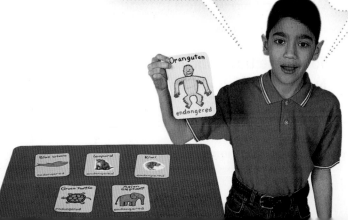

Unit 5

I can do it!

Unit 5

Performance assessment
See Assessment Package pp. 1–4, 11, 20 and 25–26.

61

6 In the Old Days

1 Read. Listen and sing.

Way Back Then

Way back then, a long time ago,
life was different, life was slow.

When people wanted to have a talk,
they couldn't phone. They used to walk.

There were no phones, not even one.
How did people get anything done?

(Chorus)

They used to ride by carriage and horse.
It took them days to arrive, of course.

When people wanted to read at night,
they used to do it by candlelight.

Today we have such different ways.
Now we do quickly what used to take days.

(Chorus)

How did people live long ago?

Life in the past

2 **Listen. Point and say.**

| 1 | 2 | 3 | 4 | 5 |

Life was different in the past.

1. People didn't have running water. They had baths in wooden tubs.

2. People didn't have electric lights. They burned candles.

3. People didn't have cookers. They cooked over fires.

4. People didn't have cars. They rode horses.

5. People didn't have phones. They talked face to face.

What did they do?

3 **Look and say what people did in the past.**

Unit 6

Affirmative and negative simple past

63

TRACK B4

4 Listen. Look and read.

The way we live changes over time. Inventions often change the way we do things.

Money

The Chinese invented paper and printing. Then they invented paper money. Before coins and paper money, people used to trade for things they needed. As time passed, people began to use shells, jewels or tea leaves in the same way we use money now. People use about 140 kinds of money today.

Records

In the past, when people wanted to listen to singers and musicians, they had to do it in person. They didn't have any way to keep the music they heard. Then in 1877, Thomas Edison recorded human speech for the first time. For many years, people used to play records made of plastic on gramophones. Today we listen to music on MP3 players, CDs and on computers.

Inventions across time; simple past; *used to* + verb for habitual past

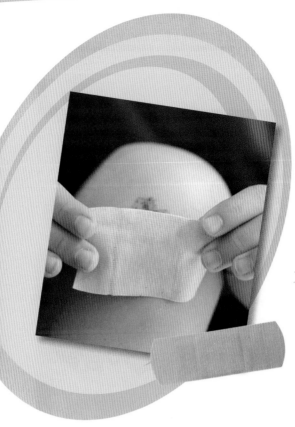

Plasters

Before Earle Dickson invented the plaster in 1920, people had different ways to stop bleeding and protect a wound. They used to chew up leaves and put them in the wound, put in spider webs, or pack the cut with sawdust. Today, we've all got a box of plasters at home.

Umbrellas

The first umbrellas were for shade from the sun, not for rain. Around 3500 years ago, people used to make them from palm leaves, feathers or paper. Later, women in ancient Rome put oil on the paper to stop rain coming through. Now everyone's got an umbrella of cloth or plastic for rainy days.

TRACK B5

5 Point. Ask and answer.

TRACK B6

6 Ask and answer.

In the past, did people have money?

No, they didn't. They traded for what they needed.

Before the invention of money, what did people use to do?

They used to trade shells, jewels and tea leaves.

Question formation; simple past; *used to* + verb

See
Grammar
Handbook
p. 116

Grammar

Did people **have** electric lights in the past?   No, they **didn't**.
Did they **burn** candles in the past?   Yes, they **did**.

7 **Complete the sentences.**

1. Did people have running water in the past?

   No, ...

2. Did they have cookers?

   No, ...

3. Did they cook over fires?

   Yes, ...

4. Did they have phones?

   No, ...

Grammar

Before electric lights, what **did** people **use to do**?
They **used to burn** candles. Now people have electric lights.

8 **Write questions or answers in your notebook.**

1. Q. Before running water, what did people use to do?

   A. ...

2. Q. Before money, what did people use to do?

   A. ...

3. Q. Before plasters, what did people use to do?

   A. ...

4. Q. Before records, ...

   A. They used to listen to singers and musicians in person.

Simple past; *used to* + verb
See Grammar Handbook page 116.

9 **Work with a partner. Talk about school in the past and school now.**

In the past, students didn't have notebooks.

They had slates to write on.

notebooks / slates ride on buses / walk

desks / benches   backpacks / belts   electric lights / candles   pens / chalk

10 **Work in groups. How is your life different now? Use *used to*.**

I used to walk to school. Now I ride my new bike.

I used to sleep in my sister's room. Now I sleep in my own room.

I used to have short hair. Now I've got long hair.

Well, I used to have just one sister. Now I've got a new baby sister.

Unit 6

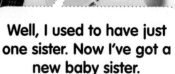

Simple past; *used to* + verb for habitual past

Inventive Ideas

The Imagination Magazine

Do you speak Doggish?

Do you want to know what your dog is saying? No problem! Takara, a company in Japan, invented a small electronic machine with buttons and a screen. It has a small microphone, which you put on your dog's collar. A translation programme in the machine changes your dog's barking sounds into words and pictures! You can read what your dog's barks mean: *Go away. I'm bored. Let's play.* Can you believe it?

WOOF!

I'm hungry!

The Top 5 Useless Inventions

We asked our readers to send in ideas for useless inventions. Here they are!

1. Silent alarm clock
2. Waterproof sponge
3. Black highlighter pen
4. Book on how to read
5. Transparent playing cards

Thanks a lot, Dad.

Olga's dog used to get wet, but not now!

OUR READERS WRITE TO US

✎ **from Spain**

A friend told me that toothpaste is 1000 years old! Is this true? – Gregoria

Toothpaste is over 4000 years old! Doctors in ancient Egypt used to

make it from powdered stone and vinegar. It tasted pretty bad.

✎ **from Poland**

Which came first – roller skates or ice skates? – Jan

The first roller skates appeared in Belgium in 1759. The inventor,

Joseph Merlin, designed them to look like the ice skates of his time.

So ice skates came first, and then roller skates.

✎ **from Turkey**

Who invented the yo-yo? – Leyla

The Chinese invented the yo-yo about 3000 years ago. They made

their yo-yos from ivory and silk cord. But the name yo-yo isn't

Chinese. It is a word in Tagalog, a language of the Philippines.

TRACK B8

11 Listen. Write T for *true* and F for *false* in your notebook.

TRACK B9

12 Listen. Read and chant.

Tell Us, Grandpa

You want to know what life was like?
Let's see if you can tell.
I used to bring Mum water
   from our family well.

I used to walk two miles to school
   in sun or snow or rain.
I copied maths onto my slate
   and then walked home again.

After school my friends and I
   had some time for fun.
We used to roll a hoop along
   or fly our kites or run.

On sunny days we used to have
   picnics by the stream.
I tell you, kids, life back then
   was special, like a dream.

Listening for the main idea and details;
habitual past; stress, rhythm and intonation

Then and Now Poster

Talk about the past and the present.

A long time ago, people used to comb their hair with fish bones.

Now we use plastic combs.

Content connection: social studies; art

Be Creative

Read and discuss.

Hi, I'm Paul. My desk used to be a big mess! I couldn't find things I needed, and I didn't have any place to keep my backpack or school supplies. I didn't like to do my homework at my desk.

To solve my problem, I nailed a hook and some empty cans to a piece of wood. I hung the wood on my wall, and then I used the hook for my backpack and the cans for my school supplies.

1. Paul had a creative solution for his problem. Are you creative?

2. What are some ways you can be creative?

3. Who is the most creative person you know? How is this person creative?

Know It? Show It!

Play a game.

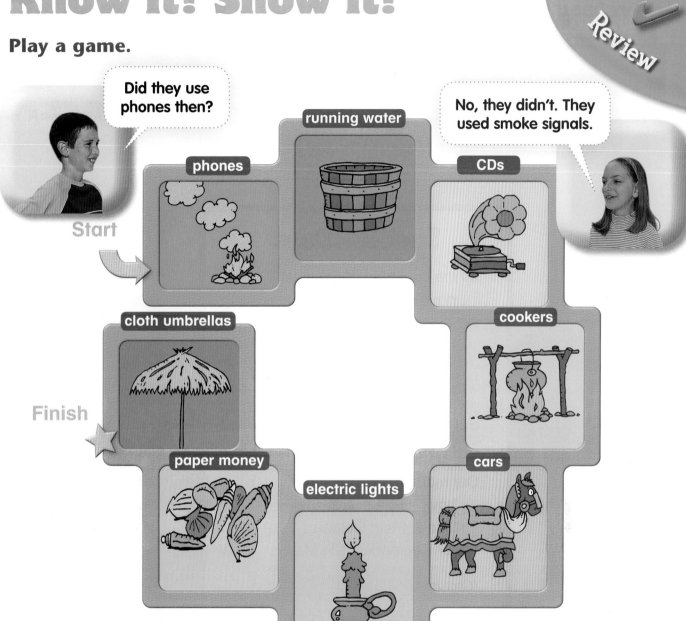

Did they use phones then?

No, they didn't. They used smoke signals.

phones

running water

CDs

Start

cloth umbrellas

cookers

Finish

paper money

electric lights

cars

Talk about your past.

When I was little, I used to ride a tricycle.

Unit 6

I can do it!

Performance assessment See Assessment Package pp. 1–4, 12, 21, 25–26 and 29–30.

7 It's a Date!

TRACK B10

1 Read. Listen and sing.

Special Days

All the countries of the world
*   have special days to share.*
We celebrate so many things,
*   but it's different when and where.*

In France, the New Year holiday
    is on January the first.
But if you're from Iran,
    it's March the twenty-first!

Our mothers everywhere
    have their special day.
For India, it's in October;
    for Denmark, it's in May.

(Chorus)

Countries sometimes mark a day
    for independence won.
In the streets, you see parades,
    fireworks and fun.

But I'm going to wait all week
    for a day that's really great.
There's a party on my birthday,
    with presents and a cake!

(Chorus)

What's your
special day?

Cultural celebrations and events

2 Listen. Read and say.

5th Nov.

7th Nov.

2nd Nov.

3rd and 4th Nov.

6th Nov.

8th Nov.

1. Sunday, the second of November, was my birthday party.

2. Monday, the third of November, was a holiday. We visited my uncle, aunt and cousins.

3. We came back home late on Tuesday the fourth.

4. On Wednesday the fifth, I went back to school.

5. On Thursday the sixth, my class was in the school concert.

6. Friday the seventh was my parents' fifteenth wedding anniversary.

7. On Saturday the eighth, I played football. Our team won!

3 Listen. Point and say.

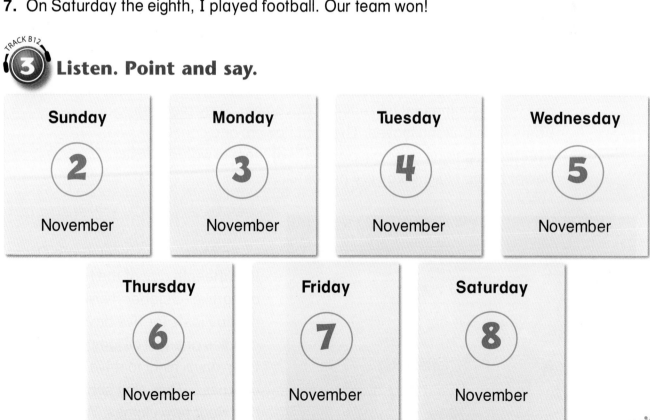

Sunday	Monday	Tuesday	Wednesday
2	**3**	**4**	**5**
November	November	November	November

Thursday	Friday	Saturday
6	**7**	**8**
November	November	November

Unit 7

Ordinal numbers; simple past

4 Listen. Look and read.
TRACK B14

Countries celebrate many holidays. One kind of holiday is a festival of light.

In Thailand, people celebrate *Loi Krathong,* a festival of light and water, on the first full moon in November. They make special boats from banana leaves. They put flowers and candles inside. After they light the candles, people float them in water. These flower boats of light are very beautiful.

In India, people celebrate *Diwali* on the fifteenth day of the Hindu month of Kartika (October / November). This holiday lasts for five days. People light candles or small oil lamps and leave them on all night to drive away the darkness. They sing songs, eat sweets and wear new clothes. Women often buy something gold or silver.

Cultural celebrations; ordinal numbers; simple present

In Finland, people celebrate a festival of light at the midsummer weekend in June. They celebrate on the longest day of the year when the sun never sets. People burn huge bonfires, decorate their homes with flowers and celebrate with family and friends.

In China, people celebrate the Lantern Festival on the fifteenth day of their New Year. A lunar calendar gives the exact date each year. They light bright, colourful lanterns. Families watch fireworks and eat small, round dumplings.

TRACK B15

5 **Point. Ask and answer.**

When are they going to celebrate their festival of light?

On the first full moon in November.

TRACK B16

6 **Ask and answer.**

How are they going to celebrate the festival?

They're going to make boats for flowers and candles.

Question formation; *going to* + verb

Unit 7

77

See
Grammar
Handbook
p. 117

Grammar

When are	you they	**going to have** the party?	We They	are **going to have** it next Friday.
When is	he she	**going to visit** Diana?	He She	is **going to visit** her on the sixth of June.

 Write questions or answers in your notebook.

1. Q. When is Kim going to visit Ann?

A. She ... her on the third of April.

2. Q. When is Kim going to go to a party?

A. She ... on the tenth of April.

3. Q. When is she going to see the dentist?

A. ...

4. Q. ...

A. She's going to clean up the park on that day.

5. Q. ...

A. ...

3 **April**

visit cousin Ann

10 **April**

Linda's party

19 **April**

dentist

22 **April**

Earth Day —
clean up park

30 **April**

Plant a Tree Day

Grammar

Are	you they	**going to have** the party on the ninth?	No, on the tenth.
Is	he she	**going to visit** cousin Ann on the fifth?	No, on the third.

 Write answers in your notebook.

1. Is Kim going to go to Linda's party on the eleventh?

2. Is Kim going to see the dentist on the eighteenth?

3. Are Kim and her friends going to plant trees on the twenty-ninth?

Going to + verb; ordinal numbers
See Grammar Handbook page 117.

9 **Copy the chart into your notebook. Write your plans for next week. Work with a partner. Compare your plans.**

What are you going to do next week?

Day of the week	Activity
Monday	
Tuesday	
Wednesday	
Thursday	
Friday	

10 **A. Write the names of three friends in your notebook. Guess their favourite holidays. What are they going to do that day? Predict and write.**

Name	Favourite Holiday	Activity
Jimmy	On Plant a Tree Day,	he is going to plant a tree.
1. _____	On _____,	_____.
2. _____	On _____,	_____.
3. _____	On _____,	_____.

B. Now ask those friends. Did you guess correctly?

What's your favourite holiday?
What are you going to do that day?

Day by Day

The Magazine that Celebrates Every Day

Birthday Traditions Around the World

Our Readers Respond
Here are some of the birthday traditions you described.

✦ People pull on your earlobe, one pull for each year.
(Maria, Brazil)

✦ Your nose gets greased with butter.
(Tom, Canada)

✦ We have noodles for lunch, and everyone wishes you a long life.
(Ping, China)

✦ You are blindfolded and have to break a piñata. Everyone shares the treats.
(José, Argentina)

✦ You get a birthday pie, not a cake.
(Vladimir, Russia)

✦ Your friends sing "Happy Birthday" to you and give you presents.
(Amy, UK)

✦ You wear a colourful dress and hand out chocolates at school.
(Deepa, India)

✦ Birthday cake candles are lit at sunrise and burn all day. At dinner, you blow out the candles.
(Katrina, Germany)

Silly Billy

When does Friday come before Thursday?

I don't know. When?

In the dictionary!

Ask Holly Day

Dear Holly,

I want to give my mother something special for Mother's Day, but I haven't got any money. What can I do to surprise her?

Alma, Krakow

Dear Alma,

Here's an idea you can try. Make a book of tickets. Each "ticket" describes one special thing you will do for your mother. For example, you can make a ticket that says Good for one Trip to the Shop, or a ticket that says Good for one Housecleaning, or a ticket that says Good for a Hug and a Kiss. Make about 10 or 12 tickets for different things that you know your mother will like. Staple them into a ticket book with a cover. Decorate the cover of your ticket book. Tell your mother to take out a ticket when she wants something. Take the ticket and do what it says. Your mother will be surprised, and very happy, too!

Best wishes,

Holly

11 **Listen. Write the sentences in your notebook.**

1. He's going to plant an ✳ ✳ ✳ and a ✳ ✳ ✳ .

2. He's going to the ✳ ✳ ✳ on Saturday.

3. She's going to make a ✳ ✳ ✳ for his mother's birthday.

4. They're going on holiday on ✳ ✳ ✳ .

5. She has her birthday on ✳ ✳ ✳ .

12 **Listen. Read and chant.**

Earth Day

Next week Earth Day is coming.
What are you going to do?
We're going to plant some flowers.
You could help us, too!

We're going to clean the playground
　　and tidy up the beach.
We're listing things to recycle,
　　and then we'll give a speech.

We're decorating shopping bags
　　and taking them to a store.
They'll give the bags to customers,
　　who'll use the bags some more.

We're having a fair on Earth Day,
　　so everyone can take part.
We're going to help our planet.
Don't you think that's smart?

Listening for the main idea and details;
future plans; stress, rhythm and intonation

Plant a Tree Day Lantern

Make a paper lantern.

What are you going to do with your lantern?

I put trees on my lantern.

I'm going to show it to my parents. Then I'm going to hang it up outside.

Content connection: social studies; art

Celebrate Traditions

Read and discuss.

In the town of Ivrea, Italy, there is a fun but very messy traditional celebration every year. People in costumes from the past throw oranges at each other. Why? It's a tradition that remembers a battle in the year 1194.

In Julia's family, one day every year, they cook and eat food that is white. No food or drink can be another colour. Why? It's a tradition. When Julia was little, she only liked white food. Now everyone in the family eats white food on her birthday.

1. Does your town celebrate a local tradition? What is it?

2. Does your family have a family tradition it celebrates? What is it?

3. Why is it important to remember and celebrate traditions?

Citizenship

Know It? Show It!

Work with a friend. Answer these questions. The answers are at the bottom of the quiz. Don't look until you finish!

1. What is the name of the festival of light in China?

    a) Candle Festival

    b) Lantern Festival

    c) Firework Festival

2. What do they eat during the Chinese festival of light?

    a) bean paste

    b) small dumplings

    c) pea soup

3. How long is the Diwali holiday?

    a) 15 days

    b) 1 day

    c) 5 days

4. In Finland, when is the longest day?

    a) in June

    b) in December

Answers
1b) 2b) 3c) 4a)

Make a calendar of your special days.

A very special day for me was 12th July. I won first place in swimming that day.

My Special Days

★ January the first — New Year's Day
★ March the fifth — My Birthday
★ May the fifteenth — Mother's Day
★ June the fifteenth — Father's Day
★ July the twelfth — Swimming Prize
★ October the thirteenth — My Baby Sister's Birthday

Unit 7

I can do it!

Performance assessment
See Assessment Package pp. 1–4, 13, 22 and 25–26.

TRACK B20

1 Read. Listen and sing.

Hobbies

It's exciting to have a hobby.
Hobbies are lots of fun.
You can take photos or build model planes.
There are hobbies for everyone.

Some people draw or paint.
    Others watch stars at night.
You can make jewellery or sew your clothes,
    or even make your own kite.

It's fun to look for and swap
    cards or shells or rocks.
You never know what you will find.
Some people fix old clocks.

Collections of marbles are good,
    but comic books are better.
Collecting stamps is always the best
    if you need to post a letter.

It's such fun to have a hobby.
There's a perfect one for you.
Try some interesting new ones,
    and you'll love your hobby, too.

What's your hobby?

2 Listen. Read and say.

John: This hobby fair is really cool! Did you see the model car collection over there?

Helen: Yeah. I liked the antique cars best. They were great.

Olga: I liked the jewellery. It's exciting to see the kinds you can make yourself.

Helen: I used to make jewellery, but now I like writing stories and poems.

John: Writing is too hard. It's fun making or collecting things. I like collecting coins.

Olga: Really? I think collecting coins is boring.

Helen: Well, in my opinion it's interesting. You can really learn a lot.

3 Point and say. What do you think?

It's hard
It's fun
It's boring
It's exciting
It's cool

It's + adjective + gerund

TRACK B23

4 Listen. Look and read.

People with hobbies have fun and learn a lot, too.

Building Models

Putting together models is good fun, but it takes a lot of patience. You have to make sure every little piece is in the right place. The worst thing is losing a piece! The best part is the finished model, when you can step back and see that it looks exactly like the real thing.

Card Collections

I like collecting all kinds of sports cards. I've got the largest collection of football, baseball and tennis stars in my class. At school, my friends and I swap cards. At home, I look for valuable cards on the Internet. A sports card is valuable when it is in good condition. An old or rare card is great, too. The older and rarer the card, the better it is.

Hobbies; comparison of adjectives

Making Jewellery

Making jewellery is a wonderful hobby. I like making badges, rings, necklaces and bracelets. I use beads, leather and other things. The prettiest necklace I made has got beads of different colours and coins in it. I gave it to my sister for her birthday. The best thing about making jewellery is that you have fun and then you can give your work as presents.

Key Ring Collections

I think it's really fun collecting key rings. I started collecting key rings when I went on trips with my family. Now my collection is bigger because I look for special kinds of key rings, such as dinosaurs or cartoon characters. The best way to store a collection is to hook the key rings on to a long piece of chain. That's the easiest way to organise them.

TRACK B24

5 **Point. Ask and answer.**

> What is his hobby?

> He builds models.

TRACK B25

6 **Point and describe.**

> Tell me about his hobby.

> It's really fun, but it takes a lot of practice.

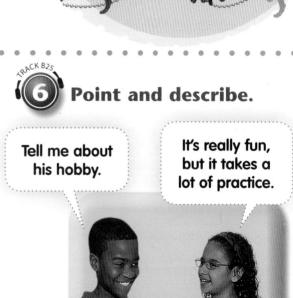

Unit 8

Question formation; comparison of adjectives

89

See Grammar Handbook p. 118

Grammar

Mike has got a **big** sports card collection.
Linda's collection is **bigger than** Mike's collection.
Harry has got **the biggest** sports card collection in his class.

Complete the sentences.

small – smaller – smallest   old – older – oldest

Kathy has got a small coin collection.

1. Fred's collection is * * * than Kathy's.

2. Sam has got the * * * coin collection of all.

Kathy has got an old coin in her collection.

3. Fred's coin is * * * than Kathy's.

4. Sam has got the * * * coin of all.

Grammar

David's model ships are **good**.
Pat's model ships are **better than** David's.
Wanda's model ships are **the best** of all.

My drawings are **bad**.
My sister's drawings are **worse than** my drawings.
My little brother's drawings are **the worst** of all.

Complete the sentences.

Mona's paintings are good.

1. Kim's paintings are * * * than Mona's.

2. Howard's paintings are the * * * of all.

John's photos are bad.

3. Vera's photos are * * * than John's.

4. Don's photos are the * * * of all.

Regular and irregular comparisons
See Grammar Handbook page 118.

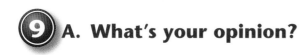

9 A. What's your opinion?

Which is the best hobby? Which is the worst hobby?
Order the hobbies from 1 to 8. (1 = best hobby; 8 = worst hobby)

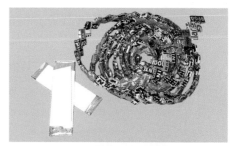

sweet-wrapper collecting

knitting

rubber band collecting

card collecting	knitting
key ring collecting	sweet-wrapper collecting
building models	gardening
making jewellery	rubber band collecting

gardening

B. Work with a partner. Compare your opinions.

10 Talk about your hobbies in a group.

I collect comics.

I haven't really got a hobby, but I want one!

I think chess is an exciting hobby. I really like it.

Irregular comparisons of *good/bad*; hobbies

Hobby Hour

The Magazine for Hours of Fun

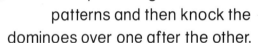

If you want an exciting new hobby, then try domino topples! You can do it by yourself, or you can begin with a group of friends. You can start with a simple line of dominoes, and after some practice, you can try longer lines and then harder designs. Children all over the world hold special domino topples in their schools or communities. One of the best domino experts is Scott Suko. He teaches children how to set up the longest and hardest patterns and then knock the dominoes over one after the other.

Scott Suko

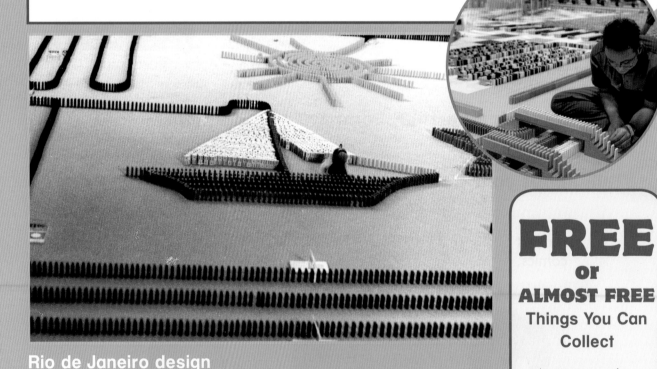

Rio de Janeiro design

World's **Craziest** Collections

Largest fridge magnet collection
Louise Greenfarb of Las Vegas, Nevada, USA, has got 29,000 fridge magnets.

Biggest hotel sign collection
Jean François Vernetti of Switzerland has got 2915 different "Do Not Disturb" signs from 131 different countries. He changes hotels often and gets a lot of sleep.

Longest chewing gum-wrapper chain
Gary Duschl of Ontario, Canada, collected 1,313,076 wrappers to make a chain that measures 17,030 metres and weighs 332 kilos. He chews a lot of gum.

Guinness Book of World Records

ASK Cal the Collector

Dear Cal,
I like collecting Olympic badges. Right now, I've got 20. It's no fun keeping them in a box. How can I show them off?

Badge Fan

Dear Badge Fan,
Wear your Olympic badges on a jacket or on an Olympic cap or T-shirt! You could also pin them to your bedroom curtains or onto a special pillow.

So what do you collect?

STAMPS

This Month's Contest

Build a house of cards!

Take a photo and show your friends!

TRACK B27

11 **Listen and match. Write the letters in your notebook.**

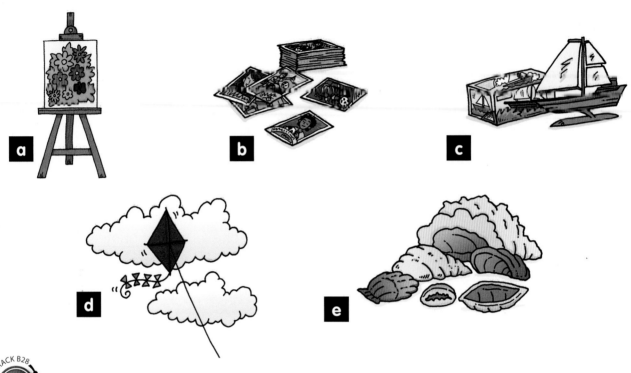

a

b

c

d

e

TRACK B28

12 **Listen. Read and chant.**

My Collections

I've got a box for big things
and another one for small.
And when I need more space,
I hang things on my wall.

My boxes are so full,
I can't find what I need.
I've also got more comic books
than I can ever read.

I've got lots of marbles
rolling around my floor.
And so many stuffed animals
I cannot close my door!

stuff

STAMPS

Listening for the main idea and details;
hobbies; stress, rhythm and intonation

Class Book

Make a class book about hobbies.

Here is a new hobby
I want to try. It's called balloon
modelling. You shape balloons to
make animals and other things.
I think it's exciting!

Balloon
Modelling

Rubber
Stamping

Content connection: social studies; art

Develop New Interests

Read and discuss.

People everywhere like trying new and different things. Learning something new helps people to develop their personalities. It also provides them with experiences they wouldn't otherwise have. A new interest is always a good way to make new friends, too.

What are some examples of new and different interests? Hobbies are a good place to start. Activities such as sports, travel, learning another language and learning how to play a musical instrument are exciting, too. Trying one or more of these activities can bring a new sense of accomplishment and satisfaction.

1. Do you like trying new things? Why or why not?

2. Describe one new activity you would like to try soon.

3. How can trying a new hobby or other activity help you?

Know It? Show It!

Play a game.

What do you think of collecting stamps?

I think it's boring.

Talk about your hobby.

I like making button people from my collection. This is my tallest doll.

Unit 8

I can do it!

Performance assessment
See Assessment Package pp. 1–4, 14, 23 and 25–26.

9 Let's Dance!

1 **Read. Listen and sing.**

Dance Lessons

Welcome to our dance school.
What would you like to learn?
You could learn flamenco
    and stamp and clap and turn.

You could learn the samba
    and maybe do the twist.
Would you like to salsa?
You can. It's on our list!

Come and take a chance!
We're going to teach you how to dance.
Footwork, arms and stance!
We're going to teach you how to dance.

We have polka lessons.
You can jitterbug and swing.
Ballet is very popular,
    and tap is quite the thing.

Many people learn to waltz,
    others learn to tango.
But perhaps you would prefer
    to learn jazz or mambo.

(Chorus)

Do you like dancing?

2 Listen. Read and say.

Mark: Hi, Jane. I'm glad you came to my party.

Jane: It was nice of you to invite me.

Mark: Would you like to dance?

Jane: Oh, no thanks. Let's just listen to the music.

Mark: Don't you like dancing?

Jane: I don't know how to dance.

Mark: Would you like to learn?

Jane: I'd love to!

Mark: Well, I can teach you some steps.

Jane: Maybe next weekend.

Mark: Why wait? Let's start now!

3 Listen and point.

TRACK B33

4 Listen. Look and read.

Dances of different kinds are popular all around the world.

Scottish Country Dancing

At the International Music Festival, I watched a traditional dance from Scotland. The dancers made a pattern of lines, squares and circles with their feet. The men wore skirts made out of a special material called tartan. They danced a dance called the "Highland Fling". They jumped up in the air and raised their arms.

Flamenco

I watched a woman dancing Flamenco. This is a traditional dance from southern Spain. The woman wore a beautiful dress and she moved very gracefully in time to the music. She sang a Spanish song while she danced. The audience clapped in time to the music and shouted and snapped their fingers while they watched.

Dance as culture

Greek Line Dance

I saw some Greek dances. This kind of dancing is lively and quick, and the dancers are full of energy. They dance in a line. Towards the end, the music gets faster and faster, and the dancers move faster to the music. I'd love to learn these dances. What fun!

English Folk Dance

I saw a folk dance. I think folk dances are old-fashioned, but fun. There is always a caller who tells the dancers which dance step is next. The caller says things like, "Turn your partner with the right hand around." The dancers do what the caller says in time to the music, and all at the same time! I like watching folk dancing, and I'd like to try it!

TRACK B34

5 Point. Ask and answer.

What does she think of the Greek line dance?

She thinks it's lively.

TRACK B35

6 Ask and answer.

Would you like to learn how to folk dance?

Yes, I would.

See
Grammar
Handbook ➤ p. 119

Grammar

| What **does** she **think of** Spanish dancing? | She **thinks** it's graceful. |
| What **do** you **think of** Spanish dancing? | I **think** it's too difficult. |

 Write sentences in your notebook.

	folk dancing	**Greek dancing**	**Spanish dancing**
Kara	old-fashioned	exciting	fast
Jim	fun	hard	noisy

1. What does Kara think of folk dancing?

2. What does Jim think of Spanish dancing?

3. What does Jim think of Greek dancing?

4. What does Kara think of Spanish dancing?

Grammar

| **Would** | you
they | **like** to learn how to dance? | Yes,
No, | I
they | **would.**
wouldn't. |
| **Would** | he
she | **like** to learn how to dance? | Yes,
No, | he
she | **would.**
wouldn't. |

8 **Write questions or answers in your notebook.**

1. Q. Would you like to learn how to disco dance?

A. Yes, ...

2. Q. Would Jerry like to learn how to tango?

A. No, ...

3. Q. ...

A. Yes, Anna would like to learn how to folk dance.

4. Q. ...

A. No, George wouldn't like to learn how to jazz dance.

Opinions with *think of/think; would* + verb
See Grammar Handbook page 119.

9 **What can you do? Talk to a friend.**

snap fingers

clap

kick

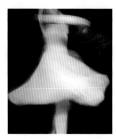
turn

10 **Copy the chart. Ask three friends. Tell the class.**

What dance would you like to learn?

I'd like to learn a Spanish dance. I think it's beautiful.

Greek dance

polka

line dance

Name	What dance would he or she like to learn?	Why
David	He'd like to learn flamenco.	He'd like to clap his hands and stamp his feet.
1.		
2.		
3.		

Ability with *can/can't*; *would* + verb + infinitive

Let's Dance

MAGAZINE

Rising Star

Prague, Czech Republic – Eleven-year-old Olga Špidla is going to study dance at the Universal Dance Academy this summer. Judges chose her as one of 300 to go – out of a total of 1000 contestants.

Here's what Olga had to say about dance. "Dance is fun. Dance makes me feel happy and strong. I feel different when I dance."

Dances Around the World
This Month: Morris Dance

The Morris Dance is a traditional English dance. Morris dancers dance in the open air at fairs and festivals. They wear white shirts and trousers and they have bells around their ankles. They make a lot of noise when they jump in the air and stamp on the ground. They dance with hankies or sticks, which they hit together, and sometimes they jump over the sticks.

A group of Morris dancers

Dancing Is Popular Again

And Everybody Loves It!

Would you like to learn a dance that's exciting and fun? It's called the polka. It's easy to learn, and the music is great, too! You can wear what you like, but some people like getting dressed up. Have fun!

Can you dance?

Here are some dance steps for a dance called the waltz.

Learn the waltz

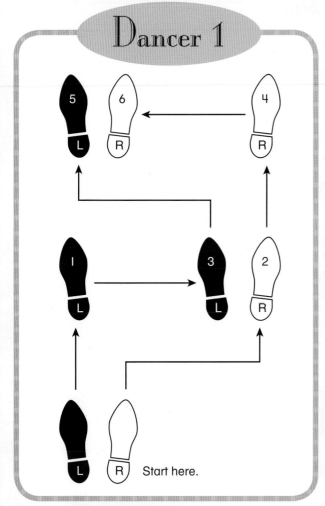

Dancer 1

Start here.

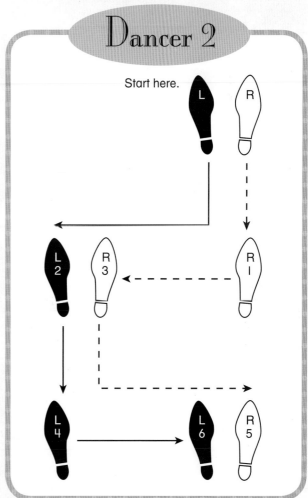

Dancer 2

Start here.

11 **Listen and match. Write the letters in your notebook.**

a

b

c

d

e

12 **Listen. Read and chant.**

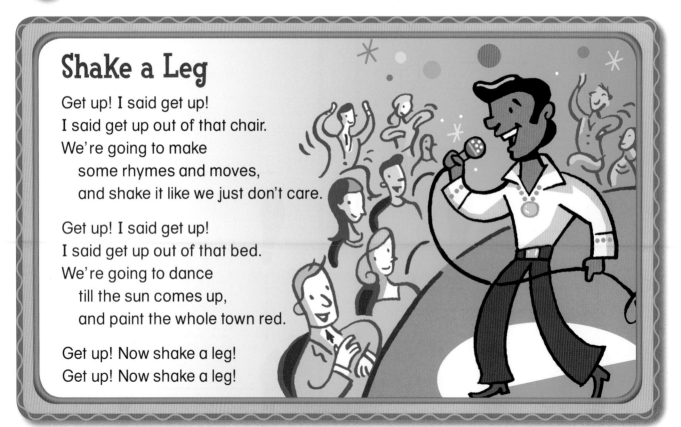

Shake a Leg

Get up! I said get up!
I said get up out of that chair.
We're going to make
   some rhymes and moves,
    and shake it like we just don't care.

Get up! I said get up!
I said get up out of that bed.
We're going to dance
   till the sun comes up,
    and paint the whole town red.

Get up! Now shake a leg!
Get up! Now shake a leg!

TRACK B37

TRACK B38

Listening for the main idea and details;
stress, rhythm and intonation

Traditional Folk Dance

Do a report on a traditional folk dance.

People dance the Sardana in Catalonia, Spain. It's a circle dance. Everybody can join in with the dancers.

Oh, that's interesting. Would you like to learn to dance the Sardana?

Appreciate the Arts

Read and discuss.

Learning to appreciate the arts is an important part of cultural education. People around the world express their culture in many artistic forms, including music, dance and plays. Other important arts such as painting and sculpture are displayed in public museums and galleries. Fiction and poetry are published in books for all to enjoy.

Appreciating the arts can begin in childhood and continue all through life. There are many opportunities for people to enjoy a rich cultural experience.

1. Do you like to listen to classical music concerts? Why or why not?

2. Do you like to see art in museums? Why or why not?

3. Do you like to go to plays at the theatre? Why or why not?

Know It? Show It!

Work with a friend. Answer these questions. The answers are at the bottom of the quiz. Don't look until you finish!

1. What is the name for the person who tells people the steps in a folk dance?

   a) A dancer

   b) A caller

   c) A singer

2. Which country does the flamenco dance come from?

   a) Poland

   b) France

   c) Spain

3. What do Morris dancers have around their ankles?

   a) Bells

   b) Sticks

   c) Jewellery

4. What is the name of the special dance they have in Greece?

   a) Polka

   b) Line dance

   c) Flamenco

Answers
1b) 2c) 3b) 4b)

Make an ad for a dance festival.

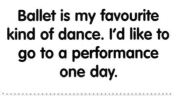

Ballet is my favourite kind of dance. I'd like to go to a performance one day.

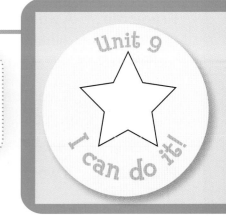

Unit 9

I can do it!

Ballet Festival

Smith Auditorium
4–10 June 8.00pm

Unit 9

Performance assessment
See Assessment Package pp. 1–4, 15, 25–26 and 31–32.

109

Grammar Handbook

Grammar Words

Adjective   A word that describes a noun or pronoun.
Linda has **long**, **curly** hair.

Adverb   A word that describes a verb, adjective or other adverb, and explains *how, where* or *when*.
Ken eats his food **quickly**.

Article   A word used before a noun to show the singular, or to show a particular or general example: *a, an, the*.
An apple and **a** banana are on **the** table.

Conjunction   A word that connects parts of sentences, phrases or clauses, such as *or, and* or *but*.
Do you want to watch TV **or** play a video game?

Gerund   A noun formed with *-ing* from the present participle of a verb.
Riding a bike is fun, but I like **swimming** better.

Infinitive   The base form of a verb and the preposition *to*.
Jason likes **to play** his guitar for children in hospital.

Noun   A word that represents a person, place or thing.
The **teacher** lost his **glasses**.

Object   The person or thing affected by the action of the verb.
Sandra washed the **plates** and cleaned her **room**.

Predicate   A word or phrase that follows the subject and describes a state or action related to the subject.
Albert **planted a tree for Earth Day**.

Preposition   A word used in front of a noun, pronoun or verb to show place, time or purpose.
Let's meet **at** 4.00 **in** the park **to** play tennis.

Pronoun   A word that substitutes for a noun.
David is a good football player. **He** is a good football player.

Subject   A noun or pronoun that comes before the verb in a sentence and explains who or what is doing the action.
Tina speaks Spanish very well.

Verb   A word that describes an action or state.
Bob **is** happy because he **visited** his cousins.

Grammar Handbook

Present of *Be*	
I am	We are
You are	You are
He/she/it is	They are

Past of *Be*	
I was	We were
You were	You were
He/she/it was	They were

Comparisons with Adjectives

- You can use the comparative form **-er** to compare **two** people, places or things.

- Adjectives with one syllable add **-er**.
  A syllable is each part of a word that has a single vowel sound.
  Examples of one-syllable words are *short*, *red*, *sad*, *tall*, *straight* and *old*.

  tall → tall**er**   old → old**er**   straight → straigh**ter**

  When a one-syllable adjective has one consonant, one vowel and another consonant, double the last consonant.

  big → big**ger**   fat → fa**tter**   sad → sa**dder**

- Adjectives with two syllables that end in **-y** also add **-er**.
  Change the **-y** to **-i** and then add **-er**.

  pretty → prett**ier**   happy → happ**ier**   curly → curl**ier**

- Use ***than*** after the comparative adjective.

  Jake is **taller than** David.

Present of *Get*	
I get	We get
You get	You get
He/she/it gets	They get

- ***Get*** has many meanings in English. In this lesson, it means *feel* or *become*.

- ***Get*** is used in combination with many adjectives.

  get + adjective: I **get impatient** with my sister.
  Ken and Sally never **get angry**.
  Lola **gets upset** when she misses the school bus.

- *Get* + adjective can have a *when* clause after it.
  A clause is a part of a sentence with a subject and a verb.
  A clause can begin with *when*.

  I get excited **when my team wins the game**.
  Larry gets scared **when he sees snakes**.

Grammar Handbook

Present of *Do*	
I do	We do
You do	You do
He/she/it does	They do

Present Continuous of *Do*	
I am doing	We are doing
You are doing	You are doing
He/she/it is doing	They are doing

- The present continuous can describe something happening now.
  You **are reading** this sentence now.
  The telephone **is ringing**.

- The present continuous can also describe plans for the near **future**.
  I'**m washing** the car for my dad this afternoon. (not now)
  Sara'**s shopping** with her mum at 4.30. (not now)

Habit in the Present

- The present form can describe what people usually or habitually do.
  What **does** Mia **do** in her free time?
  She **plays** football.

  I **read** comics.
  We all **go** to school from Monday to Friday.

- Use **how often** in questions to find out the frequency of an action.
  How often do you clean your room?

- Use adverbs and expressions of frequency to explain *how often*.
  How often does your brother clean his room?
  He **never** cleans his room!

  How often do you clean your room?
  I clean it **at weekends**.

  How often do they play tennis?
  They play tennis **once a week**.

- Adverbs of frequency come before the verb.
  Examples of adverbs of frequency are *always*, *never*, *usually* and *sometimes*.
  Sandra **always** watches TV at 5.00.

- Expressions of frequency come at the end of the sentence.
  Examples are *every day*, *on Sundays*, *once a month*, *twice a week* and *three times a year*.
  I play basketball **on Sundays**.
  Julia goes to dance class **twice a week**.
  My grandmother visits us **four times a year**.

Grammar Handbook

Present of *Like*	
I like	We like
You like	You like
He/she/it likes	They like

- ***Like*** can have an object.

    I like **bananas**.

    Susan doesn't like **basketball**.

- ***Like*** can be followed by a gerund and an object.

    I like **watching** TV.

    They like **playing** football.

- ***Like*** can combine with ***would***.

    I **would like** a glass of apple juice, please.

    He**'d like** a burger and chips.

- *I like* and *I'd like* have different meanings.

    I **like** fish. = I like eating fish.

    I'd like some fish. = I want to eat fish now.

- In restaurants, you can say ***I'd like***, ***I'll have*** or ***I want***. The meaning is the same.

    I'd like soup and a salad.

    He**'ll have** a tuna sandwich and a glass of juice.

    She **wants** a slice of pizza and a cola.

Countable and Uncountable Nouns

- Countable nouns have singular and plural forms.

    I'd like **an** egg, **two** pieces of toast and **a** glass of orange juice.

- Uncountable nouns have only one form. There is no plural.

    There isn't **any** rice? Then I'll have **some** soup.

- ***Would*** can have different meanings.

    Would + *like*

    I'd like some ice cream, please. = I want some ice cream now.

    Would + verb

    You can talk about possibility in the future with ***would***.

    Would you **eat** a chilli pepper? = Do you want to eat a chilli pepper one day?

    Would you **try** cereal? = Do you want to eat cereal one day?

    Yes, I **would**.   No, I **wouldn't**.

Grammar Handbook

Reflexive Pronouns	
myself	ourselves
yourself	yourselves
himself/herself/itself	themselves

- A reflexive pronoun refers to the subject of the sentence.

    Lucy takes care of **herself**.

    I look at **myself** in the mirror a lot.

- Plural forms have a different spelling.

    The **-f** ending in the singular form changes to **-ves** in the plural form.

    I take care of **myself**.

    We take care of **ourselves**.

Advice with *Should*

- Use *should* + verb to ask for or give advice about something.

    I have toothache. What **should** I **do**?

    You **should go** to the dentist.

    I ate too many sweets. Now I have stomach ache.

    You **shouldn't eat** so many sweets. It's bad for you.

- *Should* and *shouldn't* are the same for the first, second and third persons.

I **should eat** more vegetables.	We **should clean** our rooms.
You **should go** to bed.	You **should do** your homework.
She **should wash up**.	They **should get** more exercise.

Present of *Drink*		Past of *Drink*	
I drink	We drink	I drank	We drank
You drink	You drink	You drank	You drank
He/she/it drinks	They drink	He/she/it drank	They drank

Drink is an irregular verb. This means that it doesn't have *-ed* as a past ending.
It has one special form, ***drank***, for all persons in the past.

A: I **drink** water every day.

B: How much water do you drink?

A: I usually drink two glasses of water every day, but yesterday I **drank** one glass.

B: You should drink more water. The rule is eight glasses of water a day.

A: That's a lot of water!

Grammar Handbook

Regular Verbs in the Past	
I walked	We walked
You walked	You walked
He/she/it walked	They walked

Irregular Verbs in the Past	
I ran	We ran
You ran	You ran
He/she/it ran	They ran

- All affirmative regular verbs have the same past ending **-ed**.

    walk → walked   live → lived   study → studied

    I stud**ied** the dinosaurs.

    They liv**ed** for 160 million years, but then they di**ed** out.

- Affirmative irregular verbs have different past forms.

    eat → ate   go → went   do → did   have → had

    I **ate** a sandwich and **drank** some juice.

    Our class **went** to the museum. We **had** a wonderful time.

Question Formation

- For questions in the present, use **do/does** + verb.

    What **does** the panda **eat**?

    What **do** you **do** after school?

- For questions in the present continuous, use **is/are** + verb + **-ing**.

    What **is happening** to giant pandas today?

    What **are** you **doing** this weekend?

- For questions in the past, use **did** + verb.

    When **did** dinosaurs **live**?

    Why **did** dinosaurs **die out**?

- The verb **be** is different. For the present, use **are/is**.

    How long **is** a blue whale?

    Where **are** your brothers?

- For the past, use **was/were**.

    Was Jenny in class today?

    Why **were** you late?

- Use **why** and **because** to talk about cause and effect.

    Why did the dinosaurs die out?

    They died out **because** the climate changed.

    Why was Jenny absent today?

    She was absent **because** she was ill.

Past Forms

	Regular Verbs	Irregular Verbs
Affirmative:	I walk → I walked	I run → I ran
Negative:	I don't walk → I didn't walk	I don't run → I didn't run
Interrogative:	Do you walk → Did you walk	Do you run → Did you run

- All verbs use **didn't** (*did not*) for the negative in the past: **didn't** + verb.

    Did you **watch** TV yesterday?   **Did** you **eat** sweets yesterday?

    No, I **didn't watch** TV yesterday.   No, I **didn't eat** sweets yesterday.

- The short answer forms are **Yes, I did** and **No, I didn't**.
  Did and **didn't** are the same for all persons.

    Did she study?   Did you do your chores?   Did they go to the park?

    Yes, she **did**.   No, I **didn't**.   No, they **didn't**.

Simple Past and *Used to* + Verb

- There are different ways to talk about the past.

- Use the simple past for a single, finished action in the past.

    I **went** to the cinema yesterday. I **liked** the film a lot.

    They **walked** to the park. They **had** fun with their friends.

- Use **used to** + **verb** to show custom or habit in the past.

    I **used to have** long hair. (Now I don't.)

    He **used to play** football.   (Now he doesn't. He plays tennis.)

- **Used to** + **verb** means that the action happened regularly in the past but that it doesn't happen now in the present.

    They **used to live** in London. Now they live in Madrid.

    He **used to play** the guitar. Now he plays the violin.

- The affirmative form of the habitual past is **used to** with a final **-d** at the end.

    People **used** to read by candlelight.

- The negative form is **didn't use to** with no **-d** at the end

    He didn't **use** to exercise, but now he does.

- The interrogative form is **did** + subject + **use to** with no **-d** at the end.

    Did children **use** to write on slates?

Future Plans and Intentions

- One way to talk about future plans is to use the present continuous.

  What **are** you **doing** this afternoon after school?

  I'm going to the library. (not now, later)

  Where **are** they **going** this weekend?

  They**'re visiting** their uncle in Paris. (not now, later)

- Another way to talk about future plans is to use **be** + **going to** + **verb**.

  What **are** you **going to do** tomorrow?

  I'm going to play football.

  What **is** she **going to sing**?

  She**'s going to sing** Happy Birthday.

  Are they **going to go** shopping later?

  Yes, they**'re going to go** shopping at 5.00.

- Both the present continuous and the **going to** + **verb** forms of talking about future plans and intentions have the same meaning.

Ordinal Numbers

- The numbers we use in maths are cardinal numbers: *1, 2, 3, 4, 5* and so on.

  35 + 14 = 49   **Thirty-five** plus **fourteen** equals **forty-nine**.

  How old are you?   I'm **ten**.

- Ordinal numbers are spelled and pronounced differently. They are usually used to talk about calendar dates and steps in a sequence.

  When is your birthday?   On the **sixth** of August.

  To make chocolate milk, **first** pour milk into a glass. **Second**, pour in chocolate syrup or chocolate powder. **Third**, stir with a spoon.

- Ordinal numbers have abbreviations.

  1st = first   2nd = second   3rd = third   4th = fourth

  When you see 3rd June in printed text, you read it as the **third** of June.

Opinion with *It's* + Adjective + Gerund

- One way to express an opinion is to use ***It's*** + **adjective** + **infinitive**.

    It's **exciting watching** football matches.

    It's **fun collecting** sports cards.

    It isn't **fun making** jewellery – It's boring.

- Some positive adjectives of opinion are *exciting*, *fun*, *great*, *cool* and *interesting*.

    It's really **interesting** collecting old coins.

- Some negative adjectives of opinion are *boring*, *stupid*, *silly* and *dull*.

    It's **boring** playing chess.

Comparisons with Adjectives

- You can use the comparative form ***-er*** to compare **two** people, places or things.

    Judy is **taller** than Lisa.

    The red dress is **longer** than the blue one.

- Use ***than*** after the comparative form of the adjective.

    Ken is stronger **than** Larry.

- You can use the superlative form ***-est*** to compare **three** or more people, places or things.

    tall → tall**er** → tall**est**   old → old**er** → old**est**

- Use ***the*** before the adjective with ***-est*** at the end.

    Hiro has **the biggest** collection of sports cards.

    Mr Gomez is **the friendliest** teacher of all.

Irregular Comparisons with *Good* and *Bad*

- *Good* and *bad* are very common words, but their comparisons are irregular.

    good → **better** → **best**   bad → **worse** → **worst**

    Henry's maths marks are **good**.   My singing is **bad**.

    Lola's maths marks are **better**.   Gloria's singing is **worse**.

    My maths marks are the **best** of all.   Pat's singing is the **worst** of all.

- Use ***than*** after the comparative form in full sentences.

    Mary's marks are better **than** Alan's marks.

- Use ***the*** before the superlative form of the adjective.

    Sonia's collection is **the** worst in the class – only two stamps!

Expressing Opinions

- One way to express an opinion is to use *It + be* + **adjective** + **gerund** or **infinitive**.

    It's fun dancing at parties.

    It was nice of you **to invite** me.

- Another way to express an opinion is to begin a sentence with *I think*.

    I think Spanish dancing is really cool.

    She thinks Spanish dancing is beautiful.

- To ask for an opinion, you can use *think of* + **verb** + *-ing* in the question.

    What **do** you **think of** Greek **dancing**?

    What **does** she **think of** coin **collecting**?

    What **do** they **think of hiking**?

Nouns as Adjectives

- Adjectives are used to describe nouns and pronouns.

    It's a **Spanish** dance.   It's a **graceful** dance.

- Nouns can also function as adjectives.

    They answer the question *What kind of (dance)?*

    I like **jazz** dance.   He doesn't like **folk** dancing.

    I have a new **video** game.   She went to the **football** match.

Would like + Infinitive

- *Would like* + **infinitive** can be used for invitations.

    Would you **like to dance**?   **Would** you **like to go** to the cinema?

    Yes, **I would**.   Sorry, I can't. I'm busy.

- *Would like* + **infinitive** can also be used to ask for information.

    Would you **like to learn** how to tango?

    Would he **like to learn** how to knit?

    What dance **would** you **like to learn**?

- Give reasons for something with *because*.

    What dance would he like to learn?

    He'd like to learn flamenco **because** he wants to clap his hands, snap his fingers and stamp his feet.

- You can talk about future plans with *would like* + **infinitive** and *one day*.

    I'd like to go to a dance performance **one day**.

    They**'d like to visit** Brazil during carnival **one day**.

Writing Handbook

Steps in the Writing Process

5. Publish

Present
your work.

4. Edit

Check grammar, spelling,
punctuation and capitalisation.

3. Revise

Check for problems with ideas,
information and organisation.

2. Write the First Draft

Decide who you are writing for. Plan a beginning, a middle
and an end. Don't stop to change or correct things.

1. Pre-write

Decide what you want to write about. Collect information. Decide on
one main idea about your topic. Decide what kind of writing you'll do.

Pre-writing

1. Choose a topic.
    1. Think about your own life.

        What are some important things in your life? Do you have a new brother or sister? Do you have a pet? What are your chores at home? Did you have an accident on your bike? Did you play football and win the game? Did you win a prize at school?

    2. Think about "favourites".

        What is your favourite music? Person? Food? Animal? Sport? Place?

    3. Think about the world around you.

        Is there a park or beach you like? Do you like going to the zoo? Do you go to museums? Is there a special person you admire? Do you look up at the stars and wonder about them? Do you find interesting things on the Internet? Do you like watching birds or insects?

2. Collect information about your topic.
    1. Find information in books, in magazines and on the Internet.
    2. Watch educational programmes on TV.
    3. Interview other people about your topic.

3. Think of ideas about your topic.
    1. Make a list.
    2. Ask the "five W's": *Who? What? When? Where? Why?*
    3. Make a diagram or chart, such as a word map.

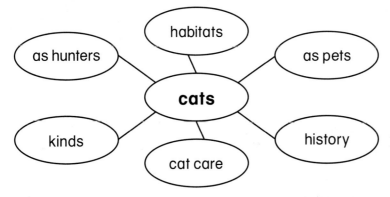

4. Decide who you are writing for: Your friends? Your teacher? Your grandfather?

5. Decide what kind of writing you'll do: A poem? A story? A paragraph? A play?

6. Decide how you want your writing to sound: Serious? Funny? Friendly?

Writing the First Draft

Now you can write your first try, called a draft. Don't worry! It doesn't have to be perfect. Just put your ideas down on paper. You can change and correct things later.

1. Put all the information you have about your topic on your desk.

2. Plan a good, interesting beginning for your writing. You want your readers to continue reading!

    1. You can begin with an interesting fact.
        Sharks can have 30,000 teeth in their lifetime.

    2. You can begin with a quotation from someone.
        "Start every day off with a smile and get it over with." (W.C. Fields)

    3. You can begin with a question.
        How much homework is the right amount?

3. Plan the middle part of your writing. The middle part should include facts and details about your topic. They should relate to and support your main idea.

    1. If your topic is sharks, then you can describe and explain characteristics of sharks. You can compare and contrast kinds of sharks. You can explain why people are so afraid of sharks.

    2. If your topic is the importance of friendliness (or smiling), then you can explain how being friendly makes social interaction easier. You can describe reactions to friendly and unfriendly people. You can discuss sincere smiles and insincere smiles.

    3. If your topic is homework, then you can express your opinion about homework. You can explain why homework helps (or doesn't help) people to learn. You can try to convince your teacher to give less (or more!) homework.

4. Plan the ending of your writing. A good ending helps your reader to understand and remember your ideas.

    1. You can remind your readers of your most important idea.
        Sharks are amazing animals, but best appreciated from far away.

    2. You can end with a quotation from someone.
        "Wear a smile – one size fits all." (author unknown)

    3. You can end with a question.
        So, how about that homework, Mr Baker?

Revising

Congratulations! You have a first draft. Now it's time to think about making it better.

1. Read your draft to yourself.
     1. Read it aloud to see if the main idea comes through.
     2. Read it aloud again to see if it sounds good.
     3. Notice which parts you like and which parts may need work.

2. Read your draft to others.
     1. Friends and family members may have good advice or ideas you didn't think of.
     2. Read your draft aloud.
     3. Ask your listeners to tell you what they liked, and what they didn't understand or what they want to know more about.

3. Look at the quality of your ideas.
     1. Are you careful using facts and opinions?
     2. Is your information from respected sources?
     3. Are there enough examples and details?

4. Look at the organisation of your ideas.
     1. Do you have a beginning, a middle and an end?
     2. Are your ideas presented in a logical way?
     3. Are all of your ideas related to your topic?

5. Look at the first draft below. Notice the kinds of changes the writer wants to make.

good beginning!

change to a complete sentence

repetition of **pile**

change order of sentence

I hate to say it, but my mum is right. It's important to be tidy and clean up after yourself. How do I know? I'm going to tell you about my uncle. I went to stay with my Uncle David in his small house for a week. I love my uncle, but he's really sloppy. When I entered, there was some sort of old or sour smell I couldn't identify. I worked it out when I saw all the dirty clothes on his chairs, bed and floor. And not just his clothes. I saw old pizza delivery boxes and cereal boxes and sweet wrappers and half-empty cola cans all over the place. I saw dirty plates piled in the sink. His dishes weren't the only pile. I saw his sports equipment was all thrown into a big pile in one corner. I saw his newspapers and magazines were all in a pile in another corner. How can he find anything? And I saw his desk had piles of papers and bills on it. How can he live like that? I know now that I definitely don't want to!

repetitive

too many sentences starting with **I**

you don't want to do what? add sentence about promising to be tidy and clean at home

Editing and Proofreading

You revise for ideas and organisation. You edit for style and proofread for grammar, punctuation, capitalisation and spelling.

1. Edit for style. Are your sentences all the same? Are they boring?

   1. Combine some short sentences.

      Bob is strong. Bob is fast. → Bob is strong and fast.

      Judy plays tennis. Anna plays tennis. Pat plays tennis. →
      Judy, Anna and Pat play tennis.

      Mark plays the piano. Mark plays the guitar. →
      Mark plays the piano and the guitar.

      Our teacher gave back our tests. She gave back our tests today. →
      Our teacher gave back our tests today.

      I like tomatoes. I don't like carrots. →
      I like tomatoes, but I don't like carrots.

   2. Check for the right word. Do you have the right meaning?
      We *one* the football match. → We *won* the football match.

   3. Check for specific words that describe more.
      Sonia is *nice*. → Sonia is *always friendly and wears a big smile*.

2. Proofread for grammar, punctuation, capital letters and spelling.

   1. Check for subject-verb agreement, plurals, verb tenses and so on.
      Linda and Fred *likes* football. → Linda and Fred like football.

      I like cows, but I don't like *sheeps*. → I like cows, but I don't like sheep.

      We *goed* to the cinema. → We went to the cinema.

   2. Check for punctuation.
      Do you believe in ghosts. → Do you believe in ghosts?
      The lake was dark grey calm mysterious. →
      The lake was dark grey, calm and mysterious.

   3. Check for capital letters.
      last month, *larry* went to *japan* on holiday. →
      Last month, Larry went to Japan on holiday.

   4. Check for spelling.
      He *recieved* a birthday *pressent* in the post. →
      He received a birthday present in the post.

Publishing

Publishing your writing is the last step. When you publish your writing, other people read and listen to your ideas.

1. There are many ways to publish your writing.
    1. Give your writing to your teacher.
    2. Make a class book or newspaper.
    3. Post your writing on the wall or bulletin board.
    4. Read aloud or act out your work.

2. A writing portfolio is a special kind of publishing. It is a place to collect your writing throughout the year. It is a history of your writing progress.

3. A writing portfolio can have different sections.

1. Collect interesting thoughts, descriptions, examples, notes to yourself and quotations in *New Ideas*.
2. Keep your pre-writing activities and first drafts in *Work in Progress*.
3. Put personal letters and cards, poems, homework or diary pages you don't want to publish in *Personal – Keep Out!*
4. Keep completed examples of your writing homework from the beginning of the school year to the end in *Finished Writing*.
5. Collect your very best writing samples in *My Best Writing*. This is the writing you are most proud of and want to share with other people.

Pearson Education
Edinburgh Gate, Harlow
Essex, CM20 2JE
England
and Associated Companies throughout the World

www.pearsonelt.com

Authorised adaptation from the United States edition entitled Backpack, second edition, by Mario Herrera and Diane Pinkley. Published by Pearson Education, Inc. Copyright © 2009 Pearson Education, Inc.

Backpack Gold published by Pearson Education Ltd. Copyright © 2010 Pearson Education Ltd.

Eighth impression 2016

ISBN: 978 1 4082 4507 1

Set in 16pt HSP Helvetica

Printed in Malaysia (CTP-PPSB)

Illustrations: Barbera, Michelle, 86, 87; Brooks, Nan, 26, 27; Burrows, Phill, 60; Catusanu, Mircea, 6, 38, 39, 70; Dammer, Mike, 25, 42, 56, 93, 115; Dresen, Kris, 3, 15, 27, 34, 39, 63, 87, 94, 99; Fasolino, Peter, 18, 19, 32; Gay-Kassel, Doreen, 10, 58, 82, 106; Hamilton, Laurie, 34, 61, 80; Hammond, Franklin, 117; Harris, Marty, 37, 58, 85, 102, 111; Hornung, Phyllis, 74, 75; Jarvis, Nathan Young, 14, 56; Kelen, Linda, 43, 49, 70, 73, 82, 97; Kizlauskas, Diana, 62, 63; Klug, Dave, 20, 30, 67, 94, 106; O'Neill, Sean, 6, 66, 96; Schuett, Stacey, 2, 3; Stefflbauer, Thomas, 13, 22, 46, 50, 51; Urbanovic, Jackie, 98, 99

Photo Credits: l = left, c = centre, r = right, t = top, b = bottom

The publisher would like to thank the following for their kind permission to reproduce their photographs:

5 Corbis: Julie Habel (tr). 8 iStockphoto: (r). POD – Pearson Online Database: Rubberball Productions (l). 16 DK Images: Philip Gatward (br). iStockphoto: JoseGirarte (bl); Shelly Perry (cr). Pearson Free Image: ©MetaCreations/Kai Power Photos (tl). POD – Pearson Online Database: (tr). 17 Alamy Images: Barry Lewis (tr). iStockphoto: Dmitry Kudryavtsev (cr). Pearson Free Image: PhotoDisc, Inc. (cl). POD – Pearson Online Database: (tl). 20 iStockphoto: Nicholas Sutcliffe (r). Pearson Free Image: G.K. & Vikki Hart/PhotoDisc, Inc. (l). 21 iStockphoto: Evelyn Peyton (br); Ints Tomsons (bl). POD – Pearson Online Database: Nigel Riches (t). 28 DK Images: Anthony Johnson (tr); Clive Streeter (bl). iStockphoto: Jani Bryson (br); Peeter Viisimaa (tl). 29 DK Images: (tl). iStockphoto: Kativ (tr). 33 DK Images: (c). iStockphoto: Rico Ploeg (r). Pearson Free Image: Dave Honor/Pearson Learning (l). 40 DK Images: Jane Stockman (br); John Garrett (bl). iStockphoto: Sami Suni (tr). 41 Corbis: Heide Benser (t). iStockphoto: Pathathai Chungyam (cr). No Trace: (tc). 44 iStockphoto: mario loiselle. 45 DK Images. 52 iStockphoto: James Thew (cr); technotr (b). Science Photo Library Ltd: ROGER HARRIS (t). 53 iStockphoto: Jeryl Tan (c). POD – Pearson Online Database: Digital Vision (tl) (tr). 54 DK Images: (r). iStockphoto: Judy Worley (c); Mike Lawrence (l). 56 iStockphoto: Maisie Ong. 64 DK Images: (br); Paul Wilkinson (bl). iStockphoto: Guillermo Lobo (tl); John Sigler (1/cl). Pearson Free Image: Dave Mager/Pearson Learning (bc); PhotoDisc, Inc. (t) (cl) (1/t) (2/l). 65 Corbis: Dave Bartruff (cr). DK Images: (c). iStockphoto: Stefanie Timmermann (tl). Pearson Free Image: PhotoDisc, Inc. (cl). POD – Pearson Online Database: Photodisc. Geostock (tc). 68 DK Images: Dave King. 76 Corbis: Barbara Walton/epa (t). iStockphoto: (b). 77 Corbis: Anna Watson (tl). iStockphoto: (tr). 88 Corbis: Gabe Palmer (b). DK Images: Andy Crawford (tl). POD – Pearson Online Database: Gareth Boden (tr). 89 Alamy Images: Blue Jean Images (tl). DK Images: (bc). Getty Images: White Packert (cr). No Trace: (cl) (tr). POD – Pearson Online Database: Studio 8. Clark Wiseman (c). 90 Pearson Free Image: Corbis (t); PhotoDisc, Inc. (b). 91 iStockphoto: (tl); Rob Cruse (cr). No Trace: (tr). Pearson Free Image: Corbis (tc). 92 Corbis: Hoge Noorden/epa (c). No Trace: (t) (b). 100 Corbis: Stephanie Maze (tr). iStockphoto: Igor Zhorov (bl). POD – Pearson Online Database: MedioImages (tc); Photodisc. Kevin Peterson (bc). 101 Alamy Images: Rob Walls (tl). Corbis: Owen Franken (cr). POD – Pearson Online Database: Studio 8. Clark Wiseman (cl) (c). 103 Alamy Images: Jack Cox in Corfu (bc); Jason Baxter (1/tc); Robert Fried (bl); South West Images Scotland (br). iStockphoto: Michael Valdez (2/tc). Pearson Free Image: EyeWire Collection/Getty Images (tl) (cl). 104 Alamy Images: Tim Graham (b). iStockphoto: Matthew Dula (t). 105 iStockphoto: Aleksey Efanov (t). 109 DK Images: Dave King (t)

All other images © Pearson Education